WHITETAIL DEER HUNTING

©1991 by National Rifle Association of America
Second Edition

Produced by the NRA Hunter Services Division. For information on the Hunter Skills Series, NRA Hunter Clinic Program, or becoming a volunteer hunter clinic instructor, contact the National Rifle Association of America, Hunter Services Division, 1600 Rhode Island Avenue NW, Washington D.C. 20036-3268. Telephone (202) 828-6240.

Library of Congress Catalog Card Number;
90-083404

Main entry under title:
Whitetail Deer Hunting—NRA Hunter Skills Series

ISBN 0-935998-90-X

HS5N5305 (paperback)   HS5N5261 (hard bound)

ACKNOWLEDGEMENTS

Authors

Mike Strandlund, Outdoor Writer and former
Program Specialist, Editorial Productions,
NRA Hunter Services Division
Richard P. Smith, Outdoor Writer and Photographer
Jim Zumbo, Outdoor Writer and Hunting Editor,
Outdoor Life
Bill Bynum, Hunter Skills Consultant, Seminar
Speaker and Vice President Sales and Marketing,
Robbins Scent Company

Editor

Mike Strandlund, Outdoor Writer and former
Program Specialist, Editorial Productions,
NRA Hunter Services Division

Production Manager

Earl W. Hower, Program Manager,
NRA Hunter Skills Department

Art

Doug Pifer, Resource Specialist, Editorial Productions,
NRA Hunter Services Division

Co-Authors and Review Committee

Merrill L. Petoskey, NRA Board Member and Member,
NRA Hunting and Wildlife Conservation Committee
Gary Anderson, Executive Director,
NRA General Operations
Jim Norine, Director, NRA Hunter Services Division
Barry Winner, Program Manager, NRA Hunter
Education Support Services Department
Robert L. Davis, Jr., Program Manager,
NRA Youth Hunting Skills Department
Dave Messics, Program Specialist,
NRA Hunter Skills Department
Doug Pifer, Resource Specialist, Editorial Productions,
NRA Hunter Services Division
Bob Belford, Program Specialist, NRA Hunter
Education Support Services Department

Kitty Beuchert, Assistant Director, NRA Women's Issues
and Information Division and former Program
Manager, NRA Hunter Information Department
Dennis Eggers, Regional Director, NRA Field
Services Division and former Assistant Director,
NRA Hunter Services Division
Mike Ondik, Forestry-Wildlife Management Consultant
and former Head Herdsman, Pennsylvania State
University White-tailed Deer Research Center
David Hale, Noted Whitetail Hunter and Call Maker,
Knight and Hale Game Calls
Jody Hugill, Hunter Advisory Staffs of Lohman Mfg.
Co., Hoyt USA, Realtree Camo Co.
Gene Wensel, Outdoor Writer and Whitetail Lecturer
Scott Williamson, Deer Biologist,
New Hampshire Fish and Game Department
Al Hofacker, Managing Editor, *Deer & Deer Hunting*

The National Rifle Association of America is grateful for
the contributions made by the preceding persons, by the
Wildlife Management Institute, and the government
agencies and organizations credited throughout this
book.

NRA Hunter's Code of Ethics

I will consider myself an invited guest of the landowner, seeking his permission, and conduct myself so that I may be welcome in the future.

I will obey the rules of safe gun handling and will courteously but firmly insist that others who hunt with me do the same.

I will obey all game laws and regulations, and will insist that my companions do likewise.

I will do my best to acquire marksmanship and hunting skills that assure clean, sportsmanlike kills.

I will support conservation efforts that assure good hunting for future generations of Americans.

I will pass along to younger hunters the attitudes and skills essential to a true outdoor sportsman.

NRA Gun Safety Rules

The fundamental NRA rules for safe gun handling are:

- Always keep the gun pointed in a safe direction.
- Always keep your finger off the trigger until ready to shoot.
- Always keep the gun unloaded until ready to use.

When using or storing a gun always follow these NRA rules:

- Be sure the gun is safe to operate.
- Know how to safely use the gun.
- Use only the correct ammunition for your gun.
- Know your target and what is beyond.
- Wear eye and ear protection as appropriate.
- Never use alcohol or drugs before or while shooting.
- Store guns so they are not accessible to unauthorized persons.

Be aware that certain types of guns and many shooting activities require additional safety precautions.

To learn more about gun safety, enroll in an NRA hunter clinic or state hunter education class, or an NRA safety training or basic marksmanship course.

TODAY'S AMERICAN HUNTER

I f you're a hunter, you're one of 20 million Americans who love the outdoors, have a close tie with traditions, and help conserve our natural resources. You know the thrill and beauty of a duck blind at dawn, a whitetail buck sneaking past your stand, a hot-headed, bugling bull elk. With your friends and forefathers you share the rich traditions of knowing wild places and good hunting dogs. Your woodsmanship and appreciation of nature provide food for body and soul.

And through contributions to hunting licenses and stamps, conservation tax funds, and sportsman clubs, you are partly responsible for the dramatic recovery of wildlife and its habitat. Hunters can take great pride—and satisfaction that only hunters know—in the great increases of deer, turkeys, elk, some waterfowl, and other species over the last century.

Your involvement with the National Rifle Association of America is also important to promote conservation and sportsmanship. In NRA, concerned hunters and shooters work together for laws and programs of benefit to the shooting sports. Most important is the education of sportsmen through programs like the nationwide Hunter Clinic Program operated by the NRA Hunter Services Division. Through the program and the Hunter Skills Series of how-to hunting books, America's already admirable hunters can keep improving their skills, safety, responsibility, and sportsmanship to help ensure our country's rich hunting traditions flourish forever.

CONTENTS
Page

WELCOME TO
WHITETAIL HUNTING

*Then the buck was there. He did not come into sight; he was just
there, looking not like a ghost but as if all of the light were condensed
in him and he were the source of it, not only moving in it but
disseminating it, already running, seen first as you always see the
deer, in that split second after he has already seen you, already
slanting away in that first soaring bound, the antlers even in that
dim light looking like a small rocking-chair balanced on his head.*

—*William Faulkner*

Whitetail deer. No other name means so much to so
many hunters. For the 12 million of us who pursue
the whitetail each fall, it means the magic of opening
morning: gray ghosts in a somber forest, filtering toward us until there it stands—the awesome image of a stately buck. It means
the camaraderie of deer camp, of success sweetened by seasons
of frustration. Whitetail hunting means companionship, adven-
ture, satisfaction, and many things only a hunter knows but even
Faulkner couldn't explain.

One in every three or four of us is successful each year—
much better success than our grandfathers enjoyed. Yet most
hunters still consider a trophy whitetail the ultimate big game
prize. That's because he's such a challenge; the whitetail may
be abundant, but he's grown abundant because of his skill at
eluding us in our own backyards.

The whitetail's keen senses and cunning are surpassed only
by his adaptability. Whitetails are the most widespread of all
big game animals. They live in the widest range and most
diverse habitats, from the big-city suburbs to the wilderness
woods. They thrive through the use of acute senses, speed and
cunning, and reproduction ability.

There are those who claim whitetail hunting is a matter of luck. Pick a stand, any stand, and see what comes by. Expert hunters know better. They know luck is a factor, but a variable factor. Each hunter makes his own luck. Each bit of information the hunter gathers and puts to work raises his chances. Good luck and bad luck each play a part, but in the final analysis, you get as much out of deer hunting as you put in.

The more a hunter knows about whitetail behavior, the better he can guess what that buck or doe will do in certain situations. A broad arsenal of hunting tricks and tactics can maximize a hunter's odds of success in any situation. With a mastery of gun or bow handling, he can finish the job at the climax of the hunt.

This book is intended to educate whitetail hunters — novice and expert alike. You can never get so good that whitetail hunting loses its challenge. But with improved knowledge and skills, your days in the deer woods can be more successful, enjoyable, and fulfilling.

Part I

Before the Hunt

CHAPTER 1

WHITETAIL BIOLOGY AND BEHAVIOR

Whitetail deer are survivors. Their biology and behavior have evolved over thousands of years to help them survive and flourish despite constant hunting pressure. The better we understand these deer, the greater our chances of filling a tag and the better hunters we will be.

Biology and behavior of whitetails during the fall is of most importance to hunters and will be emphasized in this chapter, but what the animals do and how they fare at other times of the year also have a bearing on hunting. Fawn production and survival, for example, is essential to ensure future generations of

Photo by Richard P. Smith

The whitetail deer is America's most popular and widespread big game animal. Seasoned bucks like these are among the wariest trophies a hunter may face.

3

deer. Fawns born this year will comprise most of the bucks taken by hunters next year. Bucks that survive for three years or more generally grow the biggest antlers and are the most sought of all whitetails.

Range

The whitetail deer, also known as white-tailed deer, Virginia deer, and *Odocoileus virginianus,* is the most abundant big game on the continent, an estimated 20 million deer ranging coast to coast. This hardy animal's range and population have increased greatly in the last 75 years. Decimated by habitat destruction and unregulated hunting in the late 1800s, whitetails now thrive through the help of conservation measures, improved habitat, and adaptability.

The whitetail's range covers all of the eastern U.S., much of the western U.S., and southern Canada. The deer live in the snow and cold of northern regions to the desert of Arizona and Mexico; in the deep forest, farmlands, and even suburbia. The greatest habitat provided for these "edge" animals has resulted in a strong repopulation of whitetails. Wildlife managers hypothesize that there are now nearly as many whitetails on the continent as there were when white settlers first arrived 350 years ago. In areas of prime habitat, there are probably more.

Characteristics

The grace, beauty, alertness, and speed of the whitetail is well known. Few people realize that whitetail deer consist of 17 subspecies. There is actually little difference between the subspecies other than slight variations in weight, height, coat, and antler conformation.

Whitetails range in size from the tiny Key deer of the Florida Keys, which averages about 50 pounds, to northern deer that can tip the scales at over 350 pounds. The typical whitetail is less than three feet tall at the shoulder—smaller than the inexperienced hunter expects to see.

The whitetail's sense of smell is its best developed sense and its first line of defense. Hearing is also excellent, while their eyesight is thought to be only fair. Deer have poor color vision but their eyes are well attuned to pick up movement.

When the whitetail senses danger, it usually tries to remain unseen and let it pass. It will then often try to sneak away, using its great speed, leaping ability, and endurance only as last resorts.

Photo by Irene Vandermolen, Rue Enterprises

Photo by Richard P. Smith

The whitetail's strong lines of defense help it thrive. Constant alertness and acute senses signal danger; the high-strung but shrewd deer can then run or hide from most threatening situations.

Photo by Mark Wilson, Rue Enterprises

To avoid predators, especially man, the whitetail has become primarily nocturnal. It is most active at dawn, dusk, and throughout the night, with a more brief period of activity around noon. A whitetail's typical daily routine is to leave cover at dusk, travel to a feeding area, feed and rest alternately through the night, and travel back toward a protected bedding area at first light. It will usually stay there through the day, getting up to feed and water for perhaps an hour in the middle of the day.

These characteristics will be examined closer in this chapter and throughout this book.

Fawn Production and Survival

In areas with food-rich habitat and short, mild winters, a small percentage of does breed during their first year and give birth to their first fawn when a year old. Most does not bred during their first year successfully breed for the first time when 1½ years old. In poor habitat, some does may not breed until 2½ years old.

A doe's first pregnancy often produces a single fawn. Healthy female whitetails give birth to an average of two fawns every year thereafter. Under the best of circumstances, mature does occasionally have three or four fawns.

Most whitetail fawns are born during May and June, but births during July and August are common across the southern United States. Prior to giving birth, does drive off other deer, including their offspring from the previous year, and establish a fawning grounds of 10 to 20 acres, which will be defended for four to six weeks. The major reason behind this behavior is to provide the best food and escape cover available for mother and offspring. It also reduces the chance for confusion among newborns in identifying their mother. If a fawn were to mistakenly follow a buck instead of its mother, for example, its chances of survival would be minimal.

Does do their best to protect their young from predators. They eat the placenta (afterbirth) immediately to keep its scent from attracting predators. Soon after twins or triplets are born, the doe leads each of them to different hiding places. With fawns separated, it is harder for a predator to locate all of a doe's offspring.

A doe nurses its fawns two or three times a day, remaining nearby but often out of sight the rest of the time. Each fawn is moved to a new, odor-free hiding place after each feeding. This is another behavior that reduces the chances of predators locating

6

fawns and, at the same time, familiarizes the youngsters with their mother's territory.

The behavior of fawns themselves is also geared toward increasing their survival. When frightened, fawns have a tendency to freeze, flattening themselves on the ground and lying still.

Photo by Marvin Lee, U.S. Fish and Wildlife Service

Photo by Richard P. Smith

Does usually give birth in May or June—to a single fawn, twins, or maybe triplets. Fawns instinctively flatten themselves and freeze when left alone, but depend on their mothers for twice-daily feedings and survival lessons.

Their breathing and heart rates decline to minimize movement and the chances of being seen by a predator. Spotted coloration of a fawn's coat further reduces its visibility to predators. By the time fawns are a week or more old and they become more mobile, speed becomes one of their best defenses against predators.

Fawns may nurse into the fall, but are usually weaned when 10 to 12 weeks old. They start eating vegetation when about a month old. By the time they are weaned, their chances of survival through the summer are excellent.

Winter Survival

Young-of-the-year whitetails in northern climates that aren't taken by hunters may face another test of survival during winter. In deep-snow conditions, deer may not be able to reach sufficient supplies of food. They may "yard-up" in a restricted area, quickly depleting available browse. Under these circumstances, the youngest and smallest animals usually die of malnutrition. In extreme cases, a high percentage of fawns are lost during winter, reducing the number of yearlings available during the following fall hunting season. Bucks fatigued from breeding activity are also susceptible to winter die-off.

Heavy winter loss of deer is a tragedy, and overbrowsing of critical winter range may hurt deer survival for several years. Hunting regulations are set to encourage the harvest of enough whitetails (does and fawns as well as bucks) to reduce the chances of that happening. Habitat improvement projects are also carried out by state wildlife agencies to increase winter whitetail survival.

Fawns are more susceptible to winter loss because they aren't able to reach food accessible to larger animals, and their access to food they can reach is often restricted by older, larger deer. When rations are in short supply, larger deer usually chase fawns away until they have eaten their fill. The order of dominance is called a pecking order, with the oldest and largest does and bucks being the most dominant and fawns being least dominant. Fawns of a dominant doe, however, have a better chance of getting enough to eat than the fawn of a doe that ranks lower in the pecking order.

Dominant deer often chase others away from preferred food or feeding locations by hitting them with a front hoof. Two deer that are evenly matched sometimes rear up on hind legs and flail away at each other with front feet like boxers.

Severe winters in overcrowded habitat not only take their toll

Photo by Richard P. Smith

Photo Courtesy of Michigan DNR

Harsh northern winters can take a heavy toll on whitetails. When snow is deep deer gather in yards, where they may quickly exhaust food supplies. Bucks fatigued from breeding season and young deer that can't reach high browse suffer most.

Photo Courtesy of U.S. Forest Service

9

of deer born the previous spring and summer; unborn fawns are also affected by the poor health of their mothers. Pregnant does that undergo nutritional stress during winter usually give birth to stunted fawns, many of which do not survive. Research done by the Michigan DNR at their Cusino Wildlife Research Station has shown that over 90 percent of the offspring of malnourished does weighed about four pounds when born and died soon after. Fawns born to healthy does weighed about eight pounds at birth and about 95 percent of them survived.

Whitetails that live in the northern U. S. and Canada, where long winters are common, have adapted biologically to increase their chances of survival during this critical time of year. During the middle of winter, they go into a state described by biologists as semi-hibernation. At this time, the animals become less active and their metabolism slows, reducing the amount of food they require as well as conserving vital energy that may be needed toward spring.

A long cold or dry spring during which the growth of green vegetation is poor can also subject does to nutritional stress and may result in the birth of stunted fawns. Nutritional stress among bucks during winter or spring may have an adverse impact on the size of their next set of antlers. Antler development is one of the most important biological functions of whitetail bucks during spring and summer.

Antler Development

Antlers usually begin developing during April or May and are fully grown by late July or August. While growing, antlers are covered with blood-enriched skin and this skin is covered with fine hairs, giving the antlers a velvety appearance. This is why the antler covering is referred to as velvet. Antlers are among the fastest-growing tissue, sprouting as much as a half-inch per day during peak development. The velvet dries up and is shed during early fall after antlers are fully formed.

A buck's first set of antlers usually sprouts when the deer is a year old. When fully developed, a yearling's antlers vary in size and number of points, depending on the health and size of individual animals. Yearlings living in poor habitat may grow nothing more than spikes. The first set of antlers for healthy yearlings in good habitat may contain six or eight points, although the rack is usually small.

Photos by Richard P. Smith

A buck's antlers, nourished by the velvet covering, begin growing in spring. The velvet sheds, exposing hard antlers in late summer, as the buck's hormone level increases. After breeding season, when hormone production falls, so do the antlers.

Bucks develop their best racks between 4½ and 8½ years of age. The basic configuration of a buck's rack in terms of number of points, tine length, and beam length and width normally changes little after the whitetail is four or five years old. Few, if any, bucks attain that age in areas that are heavily hunted.

Besides nutrition and age, genetics plays a role in antler development. Bucks that have a genetic makeup that does not favor antler development may have small racks throughout their lives. On the other hand, bucks with genes that favor antler growth may not reach their full potential if food supplies are poor, and certainly not if they don't live long enough.

Body Size

Deer of both sexes grow in body size during the seasons of food abundance. Although the growth rate of whitetails slows as they mature, animals can continue to grow until about 8½ years old. Adult bucks generally weigh 30 percent more than does. Bucks usually attain their maximum weight during early fall and then may lose up to 20 percent of that weight during the breeding season. Whitetail bucks weighing in excess of 400 pounds have been recorded.

Photo by Mike Strandlund

Photo: Missouri Department of Conservation

Many people find antlers to be among the most interesting aspects of the whitetail. Hunters take pride in hunting big bucks and displaying their antlers. Ironically, the most massive rack on record (right) was taken from a buck killed by a car in Missouri in 1981.

The average size of whitetails generally increases from south to north across the continent, which is a climatic adaptation. Big deer are more efficient at staying warm in cold climates and small deer are better adapted for regulating their temperature in warm to hot climates. The smaller size of southern deer has been off-set in some areas by man through the transplant of northern whitetails to southern states.

Subspecies

Seventeen subspecies of whitetails have been recognized across North America, with the smallest varieties being the Key, Carmen Mountains, and Coues whitetails, all of which live in southern extremes of the U. S. Key deer, found only in the Florida Keys, are totally protected because they are endangered due to human encroachment on their habitat. Carmen Mountains whitetails are named after the mountain range they inhabit in southwest Texas. Coues deer are also called Arizona whitetails because they reside mainly in the southern half of that state. Their range also includes northern Mexico and southwest New Mexico. Northern woodland, Dakota, and northwest whitetails are among the largest subspecies. The northern woodland variety is distributed from Minnesota and the southeast corner of Manitoba eastward to the coast. Their range extends as far south as Illinois. Dakota whitetails are spread across Alberta, Saskatchewan, and southwest Manitoba southward into northern Nebraska and Colorado. The northwest subspecies range from Washington to western Montana and British Columbia to northeast California and western Wyoming.

Kansas whitetails reside from Iowa and the southeast corner of South Dakota south to northern Louisiana and northeast Texas. Virginia whitetails inhabit much of the southeast, from Maryland and West Virginia through Georgia, Alabama, and Mississippi. Texas whitetails are distributed across much of that state and into adjoining parts of Oklahoma, Kansas, Colorado, and New Mexico.

The Columbian whitetail, which lives along the Oregon and Washington coast, is endangered like the Key deer due to habitat loss. Florida whitetails are found across much of that state into southeast Georgia. Florida coastal whitetails inhabit the western part of the state, with their range crossing the borders of Georgia, Alabama, and Mississippi. Avery Island whitetails are found along the Louisiana and Texas coasts. The final four subspecies of whitetails are also named after the islands they inhabit off the Georgia and South Carolina shore. They are the Blackbeard, Hilton Head, Hunting, and Bull's Islands subspecies.

There are only subtle differences in appearance, such as coat color and body size, from one subspecies of whitetail to another. The whitetails that live near you look similar to those found throughout the animal's range.

Subspecies of whitetails living in the northern U. S. and Canada exhibit another biological adaptation for survival during long winters that may not be as well developed in southern subspecies. As fall approaches and the amount of sunlight diminishes, layers of fat begin developing on their bodies. This fat represents stored energy that could be life-saving in times of food shortage. The more fat these deer store in the fall, the better their chances of survival during a tough winter. The scientific term for the layering of fat on whitetails is lipogenesis.

Fall Feeding

Even though lipogenesis is minimal in southern whitetails, all subspecies spend a lot of time feeding during the fall to meet increased energy demands brought on by the onset of colder weather. Periods of activity are concentrated during hours early and late in the day, but deer may feed at any time and are more apt to eat at irregular times before and after stormy weather. Does, fawns, and yearling bucks are often seen in association with one another during late summer and early fall. Mature

Photo by Richard P. Smith

Photo Courtesy South Carolina Wildlife and Marine Resources Dept.

Whitetails take advantage of all types of herbaceous foods. They graze on grasses and crops (left) and browse on buds, leaves, and twigs.

bucks sometimes form bachelor groups during the summer and remain together into fall.

Concentrations of whitetails of both sexes and various ages develop near preferred food sources. Agricultural fields of all types serve as deer magnets at this time of the year. So do apples, acorns, and beech nuts.

Although whitetails do a lot of grazing on grasses, crops, and a variety of plants during the fall, they are primarily browsers when other types of foods are not available. They bite off the tender tips, buds, and leaves on shrubs, brush, and trees within reach. Because deer have teeth only on the lower jaw in the front of their mouths, they aren't able to bite woody browse off cleanly, but break it off, leaving jagged, torn ends. By looking for this type of sign at about waist level, hunters can tell what deer in their area are eating.

Concentrations of droppings in an area are also a clue the site might be a preferred spot for feeding. Some of the types of browse whitetails prefer during the fall are willow, maple, wild cherry, persimmon, honeysuckle, sumac, witch hazel, dogwood, wild rose, wild grape, raspberry, hemlock, and white cedar.

Photo by Richard P. Smith   *Photo by Roy E. Decker*

Acorns are the staple fall food throughout all of the whitetail's range. High in carbohydrates, acorns help deer store fat for the winter.

Velvet Shedding

An increase in the male hormone testosterone is what brings about hardening of antlers and shedding of the velvet by early fall. Once the velvet begins to peel from antlers, it's usually gone in a day or two. Bucks speed up the process by rubbing their antlers on trees, fence posts, or whatever else is handy. Levels of testosterone increase during the breeding season. This hormone is largely responsible for the behavior of bucks during the fall. The higher the level, the more active and aggressive they become.

Buck Dominance and Fighting

The dominance ranking or pecking order among bachelor groups of bucks is usually well established, but they will go through the formality of ritualized sparring matches to reaffirm their social standing. More intense fighting may occur between strange bucks or evenly matched bucks that cross paths any time during the fall. Although most bucks end serious fights without significant injury, one or both contestants are occasionally killed.

The antlers of battling bucks become locked together in very rare occasions. Under these circumstances, their chance of survival is minimal. When fastened together in this fashion, bucks have been known to suffer broken necks or die of exposure. Hunters sometimes stumble across bucks with locked antlers.

Photos by Richard P. Smith

Bucks begin sparring to establish dominance and social ranking soon after their antler velvet is shed. The antlers of battling bucks on rare occasions become locked together, which usually means slow death for both deer. Even three bucks with antlers locked have been found.

The Whitetail Rut

Dominant bucks are usually the biggest and strongest individuals, and they are invariably the winners of fights. Because of their status, they make most of the sign associated with the rut — rubs and scrapes. Rubs are saplings or trees on which bucks peel or

Photo by Kenneth J. Forand

Photo by Richard P. Smith   *Photo by Rue Enterprises*

Buck behavior changes drastically during the breeding season, or rut. Bucks make rubs on saplings and scrapes on the ground, leaving their individual scent at each location. At peak activity, bucks chase does, performing the lip-curl, or flemen response, as they test the female's scent to see if she is ready for breeding.

scar bark with their antlers. Scrapes are patches of ground pawed free of leaves and other debris by a front hoof. Scrapes vary in size and are usually found under an overhanging limb or branch that may be damaged by a buck's antlers or mouth.

Rubs and scrapes are a buck's way of advertising his presence to other bucks and does. Scent from glands near the eyes and forehead is deposited on rubs. Saliva is sometimes left on limbs over scrapes, and bucks urinate over their hock glands into scrapes.

Even though a scrape is made by a specific buck, it may be visited later by other antlered whitetails, which may add their scent to the site. Other bucks may also remove any debris that has fallen into a scrape since it was last visited.

Scrapes are the primary link between bucks and does that are ready to breed. Does in heat visit a scrape and leave their scent. If the receptive doe is gone when a buck checks that scrape, he will scent-trail the female trying to locate her. Bucks check their scrapes often when in search of does. Since many scrapes are made before most does come into heat, bucks are most actively involved in scrape tending before most of the breeding takes place. During periods of peak breeding, dominant bucks spend more time with does than checking and freshening scrapes.

Bucks don't always go directly to scrapes when checking them. They commonly scent-check them from cover downwind and don't bother to approach a scrape if a doe hasn't been there. Not all scrapes made by dominant bucks are revisited on a regular basis. Researchers have found that these bucks may only maintain a little over half of the scrapes they make. Larger-than-normal scrapes and those clustered along regular travel routes or in heavy cover are most likely to be revisited. Although dominant bucks make most of the scrapes and rubs in their respective ranges, other bucks leave some of the same types of sign. Dominant males also start making buck sign earlier in the fall than subordinates.

As inexperienced breeders unfamiliar with rutting activity, yearling bucks generally make fewer rubs and scrapes than older males. The rubbing and scraping they do is instinctive behavior, but they are less likely to return to scrapes, revisiting about 40 percent of those they make.

While this is typical whitetail breeding behavior, deer activity during the rut may be greatly influenced by hunting pressure and the buck/doe ratio. If there are few breeding bucks in relation to the number of does, deer may forego much of the ritualism. The fewer bucks spend more time breeding.

18

Photo by Richard P. Smith

Hunters who locate primary scrapes—centers of whitetail breeding activity—have found a choice hunting site. Here, a hunter examines a branch where a buck has left scent from facial glands and saliva. These overhanging branches are always present at primary scrapes.

In the northern part of their range, most does are bred during November, with some bred in October and others in December. To the south, breeding may be concentrated during December and January. Prime-age does are usually the first to conceive and young does the last.

Peak breeding among whitetails is usually timed for best survival of the young. With a gestation period of about seven months

(200 days), most fawns are born when the weather and food supply are best. They are normally born early enough in the year that many of them are able to grow to a size that helps them make it through winter.

Once does come into heat, they are fertile for about 24 hours. If not bred within that time, they will recycle at intervals of 21 to 28 days until they successfully mate with a buck. Unhealthy or late-maturing does may not come into heat (estrus) until a month or two later than normal, leading to the birth of fawns at less-than-optimum times and reducing their chances of survival. One buck will breed as many does as possible, but if there are too many does for the available bucks to service, some late breeding will occur, which means those fawns will be born late and be small when winter arrives.

The female hormone estrogen increases in does as they go into estrus, which in turn increases their level of activity. Increased activity among does while in estrus is a biological adaptation geared toward optimizing the chances of does pairing with bucks during the critical hours when they are fertile. Testosterone likewise keeps bucks active during peak periods of breeding. Antlered whitetails spend little time resting and eating during these critical periods, staying on the move, which makes them more vulnerable to hunters.

Photo: Illinois Department of Conservation   **Photo by Bill Bynum**

In the earlier stages of the rut, hunters can take advantage of a buck's aggressive behavior. "Rattling," or banging antlers together, can lure curious deer, especially a dominant buck wondering who is fighting over his turf.

Establishing Ranges

When 1½ years old, most bucks disperse from the home range of their mothers in an effort to establish a territory of their own. They may travel anywhere from two to 20 miles in the process. Dispersal of yearling bucks is nature's way of preventing inbreeding, and it is also why these young bucks are vulnerable to hunters. They are on their own for the first time and may be in unfamiliar terrain.

Yearling does, on the other hand, frequently establish a home range adjacent to their mother's. For this reason, it isn't unusual for several generations of does to associate with one another during fall and winter.

Communication

Whitetails communicate with one another vocally as well as by scent and sight. Bucks trailing does during the rut frequently make a guttural grunting sound, for example, that is perhaps a way of getting a doe's attention. Bucks and does call to one another, too, but most vocalizations probably occur between does and their fawns. Fawns that are looking for their mothers frequently bleat softly. When in danger, their calls are louder and higher pitched. Does make a variety of sounds to communicate with their offspring, but these sounds are made softly, and you have to be close to the animals to hear them.

Another sound whitetails are noted for is their snort, which they make by blowing air explosively through the nose. This is a warning sound made by both bucks and does when they become alarmed or alerted to danger. The sound can often be heard for a long distance and makes any deer within hearing aware of possible danger. Some whitetails run the instant they hear this warning. The deer that snorts may run immediately, too, if it feels threatened, but if the animal feels secure it may remain stationary and blow a number of times before moving off.

Whitetails that sense something is wrong may nervously stamp a front foot to alert other deer nearby. They may do this a number of times as they advance stiff-legged toward whatever has attracted their attention. The sound of a deer's hooves striking the ground hard as it bounds away from danger is another audible warning.

The waving tail characteristic of a fleeing whitetail is a visual warning to other deer. Deer that are more concerned about attracting attention to themselves, not wanting to increase their

Whitetails have several means of communication. They leave scent to attract each other (left), stamp feet to warn each other (right), and have a variety of vocalizations.

visibility, keep their tails down when departing in the presence of potential danger.

More important than vocal communication in whitetails is communication by scent, or pheromones. Most of a whitetail's scent production comes from three glands on its legs. The tarsal gland, at the hock, produces a scent used to mark territories or scrapes. Metatarsal glands, near the ankle, and interdigital glands, between the hooves, emit scent that identifies the individual deer. Urine is also used in scent communication; it denotes fear among fawns and aggression among older deer.

Senses and Defenses

The whitetail's sense of smell is the animal's best defense against danger, and for this reason, deer frequently travel into the wind so they can smell what lies ahead. When traveling in the open where they can see danger that may lie ahead, they may keep wind at their backs, enabling them to detect a hunter or predator they wouldn't be able to see. In spite of apparent wind direction or lack of wind, whitetails use updrafts, downdrafts, and other air currents to their advantage.

The whitetail's hearing and eyesight also serve as excellent defenses against hunters. Recent research has shown that whitetails have some ability to distinguish between colors, but their color perception is not developed as well as in humans and birds.

Photo by Rue Enterprises

A whitetail's
scenting ability
is its sharpest
sense and its
first line of
defense.

It is still believed deer see their surroundings primarily in black and white, with different colors represented by various shades or intensities of those colors.

Nonetheless, hunters who wear orange clothing are less likely to be spotted if they wear garments with broken patterns of orange and green or black, unless there is snow on the ground. Whitetails don't have any trouble seeing movement, so hunters who remain still or keep movement to a minimum have the best chance of going undetected by a deer's eyes.

Whitetails have excellent hearing, but they tend to ignore or accept sounds they are used to hearing. Only noises that are not normal in their environment, such as voices, metallic sounds, noisy fabric rubbing against brush, or noisy human feet tend to alarm them. The steady pace some hunters use is probably more of a warning to deer than the amount of noise they make.

Photo by Len Rue Jr.

Photo by Richard P. Smith

Geared for escape, the whitetail has great leaping ability and can out-sprint or out-endure most predators on the run.

Hunters who move in a stop-and-go fashion like deer themselves are not as likely to alert animals to their presence.

Whitetails that sense the presence of hunters often avoid being seen by flattening themselves on the ground and remaining motionless, much the same as they did when fawns. Deer may also circle around behind hunters in a sneaking fashion.

Pelage

The brown or gray coats whitetails have in the fall help them blend into their surroundings, further reducing their chances of being spotted. In summer, their coats are reddish, but deer are still hard to see. The red coats are the same color value of the green in the forest, and actually blend in.

The hair of the whitetail's winter coat is hollow, which serves as excellent insulation against the cold. Whitetails occasionally grow short manes on their necks. Some coat color mutations develop among whitetails, too. Albinos are all white and have pink eyes, ears, and hooves. Partially white deer are called piebalds and have normal-colored eyes. Melanistic whitetails are all black and occur less frequently than albinos. Since these traits are genetic, however, they may develop more often in some areas than others.

Photos by Richard P. Smith

Whitetails occasionally show abnormalities in coloration. A mottled, or piebald, coat (left) is much more common than the albino (right).

25

The whitetail's winter coat is shed during spring and is replaced by the reddish one comprised of fine, solid hairs. A second molt occurs during late summer and early fall when deer once again don heavy winter coats.

Migrations

Some whitetails spend their entire lives within the confines of a square mile, but others are migratory, shifting from a few miles to 20, 30, or more from summer and fall range to winter quarters. The onset of cold, snowy weather usually triggers whitetail migrations. In mountainous terrain, deer tend to move from mountainsides to valleys. In woodland habitat, they shift from uplands to lowland swamps where a canopy of coniferous trees provides the best protection from the elements. In agricultural areas, whitetails may move from farm fields and edges to river bottoms or the largest patch of woods and brush available.

Depending on the severity of weather and distance traveled, migrations may take days or weeks. Whitetails generally follow the same routes to and from wintering areas, or yards, as they are called in the northern part of the whitetail's range, every year. Some migration routes become major deer highways during the transition period from fall to winter.

Photo Courtesy of North Dakota Department of Game and Fish

While some whitetails may never leave a home range of less than a square mile, others migrate long distances — usually to find food or shelter.

Antler Shedding

After most breeding is complete, testosterone levels drop in bucks and this is when they start shedding, or casting, their antlers. Healthy bucks living where winters are mild may retain antlers as late as March. Some bucks lose both beams at about the same time, while a week or more may elapse between the time individual antlers fall off or are knocked off.

Photo by Mike Strandlund

Photo by Richard P. Smith

Whitetails can become overabundant in areas of good habitat. A population that is too dense can cause problems like excessive road kills (left) or crop depredation. Regulated hunting is the most effective means of keeping whitetail populations at an optimum level.

Disease and Parasites

Disease and parasites play a role in the life of the whitetail. Warts or tumors called papillomas or fibromas sometimes form. In bad cases, these growths give the animals an unappealing appearance, but they are usually not malignant nor do they affect the edibility of the meat. Fibromas are usually caused by a virus transmitted to whitetails by biting insects.

A more serious viral disease transmitted to deer by biting insects is often fatal to the animals and is called Epizootic Hermorrhagic Disease (EHD). Diseased animals develop a fever, lose their appetite, and have difficulty breathing. The fever makes infected whitetails thirsty so they frequently die near water. Before death, deer go into a state of shock. EHD causes destruction of blood vessel walls, resulting in hemorrhaging. Outbreaks of the disease have been documented in a number of southern and western states and are usually confined to summer months.

Liver flukes, brainworms, ticks carrying Lyme Disease, and other parasites also take their toll on whitetails.

27

Man's interest in the whitetail has led to much research and has aided the animal's comeback over the last several decades.

CHAPTER 2
EQUIPPING THE WHITETAIL HUNT

Photo by Mike Strandlund

High-quality equipment suited to your specific needs can make your deer hunt safer, more pleasant, and more successful.

One beauty of whitetail hunting is its simplicity. There aren't the equipment and organization problems many other hunters face: you don't need the boats and decoy rigs of the waterfowlers; the calls and camouflage of the turkey hunters; the bird dogs of the wingshooters. You can literally grab a gun and go.

On the other hand, there are several pieces of gear that can be a great aid in a deer hunt. If you've ever wished you could tell if a deer were a buck or a doe, wanted to hide from a deer's eyes or nose, or simply get comfortable on stand, there was probably a piece of gear that could have helped.

Clothing

Foremost in comfort and safety on a deer hunt is clothing. The right clothing is important not only for protection from the elements, but to be seen — or not seen — whichever the case may be.

Blaze Orange

Blaze orange outerwear is the standard for firearms deer hunters today. It is required by law in most states and is strongly recommended anywhere that gun-deer hunters may come in contact. Researchers have found that blaze orange (not to be confused with tan-orange or rust-orange) is much more visible than the old red coats of decades past. It has significantly reduced hunting accidents — both hunters mistaken for game and hunters not seen in the line of fire.

Most states and provinces have a required minimum of blaze orange that must be worn during firearms seasons. In some areas, this is only a hat, a vest, or a couple hundred square inches of material. Only a handful of states have no blaze orange requirement, and

NRA Staff Photo

Blaze-orange outerwear, crucial for optimum safety, is standard issue for firearms deer hunters. While the camouflaged blaze-orange pattern (right) is less visible to deer, it is also less visible to other hunters.

in all of those states it is under consideration. Wearing at least 100 square inches of blaze orange (the equivalent of a solid orange hat) is strongly recommended for all firearms deer hunting.

Photo by Mike Strandlund

The more blaze orange that is worn, the more visible a hunter is to other hunters. Unfortunately, he is also more visible to deer if he is on the ground in a dark woods bare of snow. The whitetail's poor ability to differentiate colors makes the blaze orange appear white; the wearer is camouflaged against snow or sky. But true blaze orange appears almost like a light source in dark woods — even to deer.

Many hunters wear full blaze orange when moving through the woods, then shed some when they get to their stand,

A still-hunter, moving stop-and-go through thick cover, needs to be even more visible than a stand hunter. A solid blaze-orange vest is minimum; there should also be some orange or red on the pant legs, and a blaze-orange cap. Check the blaze-orange requirements of your state or province.

taking care to wear at least the legal minimum. Moving through a woods, a hunter should wear as much blaze orange as possible. The full-blaze coveralls or jacket/pants are the most visible and are recommended for optimum safety.

Most hunters wear an orange hat and jacket or vest. But when moving through thick cover, it is also important to have some orange on your legs or feet. This may be orange pants, a bandanna tied above a knee, or the tops of orange socks exposed above your boots. Many of the mistaken-for-game accidents that have occurred during deer hunting were caused by irresponsible hunters seeing and shooting at only the legs of another hunter.

Camouflage blaze orange, a mottled pattern of black and orange, gives you visibility to hunters but helps hide you from deer. Studies have shown this pattern may not be as safe as solid blaze orange, however. Another way to be visible to fellow hunters but hard for a deer to detect is to wear red along with blaze orange — perhaps a blaze orange vest over a red jacket. If you are hunting from a tree stand, you're better off wearing the blaze orange, which blends well with the sky from a deer's point of view.

Outerwear

Besides being blaze-orange, deer hunting outerwear must have other properties. Depending on weather conditions and your hunting style, you may need warmth, quietness, toughness, light weight, and water-repellency.

Outerwear popular with deer hunters include insulated coveralls or coat/pant outfits for cold-weather hunting. When it's milder, hooded sweatshirts, parkas, or quilted vests are better.

Some hunters prefer their regular winter work clothes and a low-cost blaze-orange vest. Avoid the cheap vinyl vests you can buy for about a dollar; they crackle and tear with the slightest movement when it's cold. Spend a couple more dollars for a vest made of cotton.

In the northern tier of states, deer season can be so cold that a heavy coat or insulated coveralls are necessary to sit out a deer stand. But in most cases, hunters are better off with layers of clothing that let them adjust their insulation as weather gets warmer or colder, or they have more or less activity to keep them warm. The right clothing for comfort varies a great deal from

Photos by Mike Strandlund

Whitetail seasons may coincide with the heat and humidity of summer or the cold and snow of winter. It's important to choose your hunting wardrobe carefully.

Dressing in layers allows you to match your clothing for changing temperatures and varying amounts of activity.

the time you hike in to your stand, sit in the predawn chill, still-hunt in the sunshine, and drag out your deer in the warmest part of the afternoon. In this case, you may want more than one article of blaze orange clothing—one light and one heavy.

Wool is the all-time favorite outerwear of deer hunters for many reasons. It is very warm for its weight, even when damp. It is quiet when brushed against twigs, and it doesn't restrict movement.

Other jacket materials include cotton and nylon shells with insulation, either goose down, poly-

Wool clothing, a favorite among deer hunters for centuries, remains popular because of its quietness and warmth even when wet.

ester, or other man-made insulators. For very rugged weather, most popular now are the super-insulative synthetics combined with an outer fabric that lets out perspiration but keeps out precipitation. This fabric is noisy in the brush, however.

Reversible coats, vests, or coveralls, with blaze orange on one side and camouflage on the other, are useful for all-season hunters.

Most whitetail hunters occasionally find they need rainwear. There is a vast diversity in the quality of rainwear. Cheap vinyl rainsuits and ponchos are seldom worth the trouble for a hunter — they usually come to pieces their first time out of the bag. Rubber is durable, but heavy and bulky. Lightweight, high-quality suits made of rubberized nylon are best. They should be able to "breathe" for optimum comfort. Rainwear that conforms to blaze-orange regulations is difficult to find. You may need a lightweight vest over the rainsuit.

Underwear

Most hunters aren't careful about buying underwear. It's too easy to just go out and buy a cheap pair of cotton longjohns. They may be fine in the beginning, but after a couple of washings the cuffs have crept up your calf, and the crotch is closer to your knees than where it is supposed to be. Cotton by itself is not very warm, and if you break into a sweat getting to your stand, you'll remain damp for a long time.

High-quality underwear keeps you warmer and drier. You're more comfortable and don't need outer garments that are as heavy, which makes for freer movement.

Wool underwear is best unless your skin is sensitive to the scratchiness of wool. In that case, a double-layer underwear with polypropylene on the inside and wool on the outside is a good choice. Polypropylene and other synthetic fabrics have wool's ability to wick moisture away from the skin.

Footwear

Perhaps the most vital part of a deer hunter's wardrobe is his footwear. Boots must be warm enough (or cool enough) depending on climate; they must fit right; and they must provide good traction.

Boot soles come in a variety of designs — soft or hard, deep track or almost smooth. Soft soles grip the best on hard, rocky terrain, while hard soles dig better into dirt. Boots with deep-track soles provide the best traction in most cases, but become clogged and heavy in clay mud.

High-quality rainwear can keep you comfortable and sitting still on stand when the weather turns bad.

For colder climates, where it is difficult to keep your feet warm while on stand, a leather or rubber boot with felt or quilted pacs is most popular. These styles are made with rubber bottoms and rubber, leather, or nylon tops. The fully rubber ones are the most waterproof; nylon is lightest.

Other hunters prefer insulated leather or rubber hunting boots. These are lighter than pacs and make for easier walking. High-topped rubber boots allow you to keep dry as you walk in water and help hide your scent trail on your way to your stand. But don't make the mistake of wearing boots that are not warm enough. If your feet get so cold that you have to get out of your stand and walk around, this little oversight can ruin your chance at a deer.

Socks can make the difference. At least a couple layers are standard, usually cotton inner and wool outer socks. If you get hot and your feet get sweaty, however, this combination can be miserable. Polypropylene inner socks are more expensive than cotton, but are much more comfortable in that case.

There are several gadgets meant to solve the cold-feet-on-stand problem. These include electric socks and oversized, down-insulated "booties" you slip right over your boots on stand. These are quite expensive; you can accomplish the same thing by wrapping a small blanket around your lower legs and feet.

Headgear

Hats are designed for different functions, so it is important to choose the right type. Your deer hunt may require warmth, protection from rain or snow, shading from the sun, or any combination of these.

In cold-weather hunting, warm headgear is very important. Below freezing, over 50 percent of the body's generated heat may escape through an unprotected head. This heat loss saps extremities of warmth as the body tries to keep its core warm. Strange as it seems, improper headgear can give you frostbitten toes!

Wool stocking caps are generally the warmest. They offer no protection from the sun and little from the rain, though, and they have an annoying tendency to get caught and pulled off by brush. The balaclava or ski mask style stays on better and is even warmer. But with its full coverage of ears, it may hamper your hearing. Some hunters who wear these caps cut small ear holes in them.

It is very important to be able to keep your eyes shaded when there is sun in your face. This is most critical for hunters who wear glasses; the glint from glasses has saved many a whitetail's hide. Baseball cap styles are best for shading your eyes, and may be insulated for some additional warmth. But they are useless in very cold weather, because they offer no covering for ears.

The Jones style hat is a good compromise. While not as warm as a stocking cap, it offers better protection from wind, rain, and sun. This style is usually insulated with flaps that can be pulled part way over the ears. With its soft, adjustable brim, it is a good choice for bowhunters who find that hard-brimmed caps interfere with the bowstring at full draw.

Another favorite style among hunters is the trooper cap with snap-up insulated brims and ear muffs. This style is also available with a regular stiff front brim.

Hoods are the warmest headgear, but they can severely restrict your hearing.

Many states require that you wear a blaze orange hat. Even if they don't, it's a good idea.

Gloves and Mittens

Deer hunters have a hard time deciding which type of gloves or mittens to wear. They're faced with a dilemma: They need their hands warm and flexible, but they also need to handle a gun with dexterity.

A good approach is to wear gloves or mittens that keep you plenty warm, which you can quickly shuck when it comes time to shoot. The best ones have high-efficiency insulation and waterproof outer material. If the weather is mild and you can get by with light gloves, you may be able to shoot with them on. But don't shoot wearing gloves unless you've *practiced* shooting that way.

On stand, you may be able to remove the glove on your trigger hand and keep it in a pocket. It will probably be warmer that way, anyway. Another option is to use gloves or mittens made for cold-weather shooters, which have a slot in the palm through which you can extend your trigger finger.

Keep in mind that gloves are usually the first thing to get soaked in snow or rain. A spare pair, carried in a plastic bag, may save you from misery.

Hunting Aids

In recent years, a vast amount of commercial equipment has been manufactured to help the hunter bag a deer. Some of this gear is very useful; some is just costly, bothersome junk. Deer hunters vary in opinion on much of it. Here is some other hunting equipment you may want to consider.

Portable Tree Stands

There is no doubt that a tree stand, used correctly, can get you closer to whitetails. The problem is having tree stands at the right place at the right time. The solution is a portable tree stand.

Modern portable tree stands are relatively easy to carry and erect. They come in several designs: a simple platform that clamps to a tree trunk; a platform/seat combination that you use to climb the tree; ladder stands you lean against a tree, and more. Some are lighter, easier, and quieter to use than others. Some are safer. Try before you buy.

If you do get a portable tree stand, you will need some accessories. These include tree-climbing steps, seat, safety harness, and haul line to pull your gear into the tree with you. A heavy hook you can fasten to the tree to hang some gear is another useful tree-stand item.

Photos by Wade Bourne

Portable tree stands enable the deer hunter to have a comfortable, concealed post in just the right location. Portables come in a variety of designs, including the climbing tree stand (left) and the ladder stand.

Seats

If you hunt from the ground rather than from a tree, you'll probably spend a lot of time sitting. A portable stool or a warm, dry seat pad is well worth carrying for the comfort it provides. It can increase your chance of success by keeping you sitting still longer.

Popular seats for hunters are folding stools of heavy wire or aluminum tubing, and plastic pads filled with styrofoam pellets. They are all easy to carry in a pack or attached to a belt.

Scents

A deer uses its nose more than any other sense. A hunter can use special scents to keep the deer from detecting him, or to actually attract a deer.

Scents that conceal or confuse a hunter's body odor are called cover scents. The most popular ones include fox urine, pine oil, and other strong, natural odors. These are placed on the hunter's body, especially on boots, to hide his scent trail and mask his body odor.

Skunk essence was at one time the most popular cover scent. Its ability to overpower any other scent is indisputable. But fewer hunters use it today; research has shown that deer may be alerted by the odor. Anything that would cause a skunk to spray could pose a threat to a deer.

Too many hunters place too much confidence in cover scents. Hunters must first be as clean as possible and divert their scent

Photo by Mike Strandlund

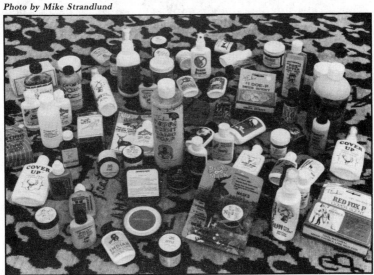

Modern deer hunters may choose from an endless array of cover scents, attractor scents, and scent-eliminating products. The authenticity and effectiveness of these products vary considerably.

by being downwind or in a tree stand. Only then can a cover scent help hide what human odor remains.

The other type of scent is the attractor. To most hunters this means doe-in-heat urine used to attract bucks during the rut. But it can also be a buck scent to attract a buck looking for a fight, interdigital gland scent to make an authentic scent trail, or any type of deer scent that appeals to the curiosity of deer.

Doe-in-heat scent seldom gets the magical results hunters expect. But there are many reports of bucks following a hunter's doe-scent trail right to his stand.

Some companies manufacture scents of apples and other food lures that supposedly attract deer. The effectiveness of these scents is dubious, however. These scents usually contain an array of chemicals that are readily identified as counterfeit by the sophisticated noses of deer. Use authentic scents that are natural to the area.

Deer Calls and Decoys

Attractor scents, deer calls, rattling antlers, and even decoys are part of the newest craze in deer hunting — that of actively bringing a deer to you. The trend is due in part to advertising by manufacturers trying to sell these products, and in part by the fact that they sometimes work.

Buck calls simulate the groaning sound a buck makes when he is on the trail of a hot doe. These calls are operated either by air or friction. Some hunters have recently reported success by using deer snort calls. Traditionally thought to be only an alarm call, the snort of a whitetail may have several meanings, researchers have found.

Rattling, popular in Texas for many years, is catching on across the country. Usually real buck antlers are used, but there are simulated rattling horns on the market. Several manufacturers make a bag of hard-plastic rods that when jostled sounds like sparring bucks.

Lifesize deer decoys have been used for hunting bucks during the rut. Some of the handful of hunters who have tried them report success, and a few tell wild tales of bucks falling in love with the fraudulent does. The main problem is transporting and setting them up in the woods.

Optics

Anyone who has taken binoculars hunting is reluctant to hunt without them. They are a tremendous aid for the deer hunter

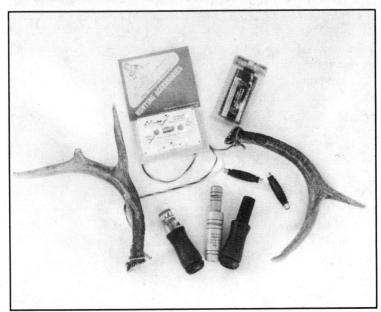

Calls, rattling antlers, and even deer decoys are becoming more popular with whitetail hunters. Hunters using these unusual tactics must be knowledgeable in deer behavior and take precautions to avoid dangerous situations.

in finding deer and separating bucks from does. You may be able to spot a deer from long distance and make a stalk. Or you can carefully scan an area for deer without having to walk it, saving time.

Compact binoculars, which weigh as little as eight ounces, are ideal for the deer hunter. Larger models offering higher magnification, field of view, and variable power in some cases, may be an advantage.

Spotting scopes provide a much higher magnification than binoculars and are designed for systematic scoping in open country. Since white-tails stay in cover most of the time, their application for whitetail hunting is limited.

Photo by Mike Strandlund

Binoculars help the whitetail hunter spot deer and examine antlers. They also save legwork, allowing you to check an area without walking there.

They are useful for getting a close look at deer on fields during dawn and dusk.

A rangefinder is another optical device of occasional use to the whitetail hunter. It tells the yardage of game so the shooter can compensate for the trajectory of his bullet or arrow. But since whitetails are seldom seen in the open, are usually shot at close range, and don't like to stand still for distance readings, few deer hunters use these gadgets.

Woodsmanship Gear

Next in importance after clothing, gun, and ammo are the items that keep you safe and in control outdoors. A pack full of carefully chosen gear and supplies will make a day in the deer woods more pleasant and productive.

Pack

First you need a way to carry your gear. You may be able to get it into big pockets, but a pack is preferable.

For a small amount of gear, a fanny pack may be best. It rides around your hips and does not restrict shoulder movement. For more gear, a daypack/backpack is necessary.

Photo by Mike Strandlund

When you plan to roam the deer woods all day, a well-supplied daypack can make your outing safer and more enjoyable.

Don't buy a pack designed to carry schoolbooks; get a heavy duty bag with tough zippers. A few manufacturers make packs of tough cotton, which is very quiet in the woods. Nylon is more durable, sheds water easily, and won't absorb undesirable odors to as great a degree. Nylon is more noisy, however.

Compass

This is an item of equipment that should be carried by every hunter, whether he is hunting remote wilds miles from the nearest road or a 40-acre woodlot near his home. Don't bother with cheap compasses; they can cause more trouble than they save. Get a high-quality model with a luminescent dial. Know how to use it, and *do* use it when you go *into* the woods. You can't tell which way is out if you don't know which way you came in.

Compasses come in a variety of designs, including those you carry in your pocket, pin to your coat, and strap on your wrist. The best models are those with adjustable direction-bearing dials and a strong cord to secure it to yourself.

Maps

Maps are also valuable to help you "stay found," and they can help point your way to the deer if you know how to use one. We're talking about topographical maps, which show elevation contours, woods and openings, and other information valuable to hunters.

To order maps, contact: Branch of Distribution, U. S. Geological Survey, Box 25286, Denver, CO 80225; Telephone 303/236–7477. Maps cost $2.50, which covers postage. Indexes to identify the maps you need may be ordered free of charge.

Photo by Mike Strandlund

A map and compass are an important part of your hunting gear. Used skillfully, they not only keep you from getting lost, but help you find likely spots for intercepting deer.

Knives

As with any type of deer hunting gun or gear, knives come in an array of shapes and sizes, and you have to decide which best suits your needs. The main function of a hunting knife is to field dress the animal. For this, you don't need a bayonet. A light blade with a three- or four-inch blade is ample, and even a two-inch penknife could do the job. There are specialized knives designed for gutting game, with a hook or blade protector that make splitting the belly as easy as undoing a zipper. They can be very helpful if you dress a lot of deer or must do so quickly. But their design often takes away from the knife's ability to perform well in standard knife duty.

A small knife usually serves the hunter best because it is light and unobtrusive. Large sheath knives are heavy, get caught on brush, and may poke you in the kidney when you sit down. They are unwieldy in precise jobs. On the other hand, a large knife may be more practical if you foresee heavy duty jobs like splitting a pelvic bone, cutting poles, or performing other tough chores.

On extended hunts, it is best to have a small knife for smaller jobs and a big blade for big ones. Be sure to bring a sharpening stone.

Food and Drink

For a full day in the woods, you'll need food and drink to keep you going. Stick with high-energy, easy-to-handle foods that don't cause a lot of noise and odor. Make sure they can't spoil before you eat them.

Candy bars seem the logical choice for many hunters, but don't load your pack with sweets. Nuts, apples, carrot sticks, jerky, and bread are better.

Drink should be kept in a reclosable container such as a canteen or screw-top bottle.

Equipment Considerations

There are several other items of equipment a whitetail hunter should consider.

A **gun rack** in the hunting vehicle can increase safety, ease of handling, and protection for the bow or firearm. A **drag rope**

Photo by Mike Strandlund

Your whitetail hunting success can depend on seemingly minor pieces of equipment, such as screw-in steps that give you access to a lofty stand.

is a virtual necessity on a deer hunting trip, and you may consider other options for transporting deer out of the woods, such as a **winch** or **all-terrain vehicle.** You may want a **hatchet** to split the deer's pelvis bone and perform general camp duties.

Some deer hunters carry a **damp rag** in a **large plastic bag.** When they shoot and field dress a deer, they use the damp rag to wash up, and the plastic bag to carry the liver and heart. In hot weather, you should have a large piece of **cheese cloth** or similar material to protect the carcass from flies and other insects.

Don't forget your **hunting license, back tag, stamps,** and **written permission** as required.

Miscellaneous tools and camping gear, depending on the type of hunt you're on, will make it smoother and much more enjoyable.

Photo by John Weiss

A comfortable camp well stocked with provisions can make your deer hunt much more enjoyable.

Here are a few other things you may want on your next deer hunting trip:

- Lantern
- Toilet Paper
- Sleeping Bag, Pad, and Pillow
- Flashlight
- Extra Batteries and Fuel
- Tent, Stakes, Stake Driver
- Camp Stove
- First Aid Kit, Snake Bite Kit
- Fire-Building Materials
- Heater, Fuel
- Prescription Medications
- Water
- Spare Clothing
- Food and Drink
- Rope
- Saw or Axe
- Spare Eyeglasses
- Cooking and Eating Utensils
- Shave Kit, Wash Cloth, Towel
- Food and Drink
- Camera and Film
- Cooler and Ice
- Alarm Clock
- Extra Ammunition and Clip
- Backup Firearm or Bow
- Gun Cleaning Equipment

CHAPTER 3
DEER GUNS AND BOWS

Selecting the right gun or bow and learning to use it well are pivotal for success in deer hunting.

The whitetail deer has been hunted with every sporting arm known to man. Centerfire rifles are today's standard, but other arms are increasingly popular as hunters and hunting situations change. Shotguns are required in more areas each year as development encroaches on hunting land — and deer encroach on civilization. Bowhunters, who until recently took only an insignificant number of whitetails, are now responsible for a considerable percentage of the harvest. Blackpowder hunters and handgunners bag more deer each year as state game agencies respond to growing interest and accommodate these guns for deer hunting. Hunters respond to these new opportunities by taking up bowhunting or muzzleloading for longer, more-interesting, more-challenging, and less-crowded hunting seasons.

Selecting a Gun or Bow

The type of sporting arm you use is purely a matter of personal choice and ability. Narrowing it down to the specific gun or bow and sighting system requires more consideration. You have to know the limitations of your gun and your shooting ability — and stay within those limitations. Foremost is using "enough" gun or bow. Enough in this context means a gun or bow that has enough energy at hunting ranges to kill surely and quickly. For example, a .30–30 is not enough gun for 300-yard shots; nor is a 35-pound recurve enough bow at 40 yards.

Assuming the bullet or arrow can do the job once it gets there, most important is that it *does* get there. The best gun or bow is the one you can shoot most accurately in hunting situations. A .243 you can shoot more accurately than a .300 Magnum is superior to the higher-power caliber. Indeed, bullet placement *is* more critical with lower-energy calibers. You must also consider the job you've asked your gun or bow to do. In one hunting situation, an iron-sighted .44 carbine might be best; in another, a .270 with high-power scope is the logical answer. Buckshot may be the best choice or the worst choice depending on circumstance.

Finally, you may consider factors other than what is most effective. You may choose a gun for sentimental reasons, or because it *is* less effective, making you get closer and adding greater challenge to the hunt. Cost of the gun or ammo may be a major consideration. You may use a certain gun simply because it is the one that is available.

Whether you own a favorite deer gun or are trying to decide

There are many types of centerfire long guns popular among deer hunters today. They include, top to bottom, bolt-action rifle, lever-action rifle, pump-action rifle, semi-auto rifle, single-shot rifle, semi-auto shotgun, pump-action shotgun, and double-barrel shotgun.

among guns or bows, this chapter will discuss some things you should consider.

Rifles for Whitetails

For nearly a century following the Civil War, the favorite arms of the deer woods were the lever-action carbines that fired rather large, slow bullets with mediocre accuracy. Those Winchesters, Marlins, and Savages certainly did the job and are still popular, especially in the East and Midwest. Since then, modern rifles in bolt-action, pump, and semi-automatic have gradually become more popular in the last 30 years. Still, it seems that no matter how many deer hunters are gathered in a discussion of the best deer rifle, there are an equal number of opinions on what exactly comprises that gun.

The fact is that the perfect deer rifle does not exist. While some may be generally better than others, each is adapted to different situations and shooters. The whitetail hunter has a huge selection of rifles to choose from — more rifles have been designed for deer hunting than for any other sporting purpose. While many of the differences in energy, trajectory, and speed of operation

Photo by S.A. Johnson, Minnesota Historical Society

Lever-actions shooting large-bore, low-velocity bullets were the most popular rifles among whitetail hunters for nearly a century after the Civil War. Today, high-velocity calibers see the most use.

have little bearing on whether you get your deer, there are some important considerations.

Calibers and Loads in Deer Rifles

The effectiveness of a firearm in bringing down a whitetail is a combination of factors. These are accuracy, trajectory (which affects accuracy) and the energy imparted by the bullet inside the animal. This energy is a function of the bullet's velocity, weight, construction, and amount of penetration in the animal.

Photo by Mike Strandlund

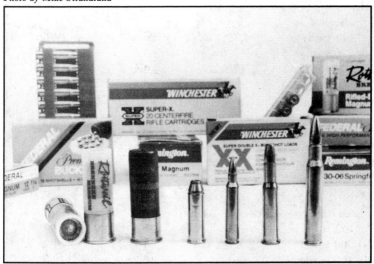

Centerfire loads cover a wide spectrum. Represented here are shotgun slug and buckshot; high-power handgun cartridge (.44 Mag.); high-velocity small-bore (.223); low-velocity large bore (.30-30); and high-velocity large-bore (.30-06). All but the .223, which has too little energy and improper bullet construction, may be used for whitetails.

With bullet placement the most critical factor, your gun's accuracy is more or less important depending on your shooting ranges. Trajectory comes into play at ranges beginning at 100 yards with some loads. Energy is critical at any range. Experts generally consider minimum energy for a whitetail load to be about 1,200 foot-pounds at the point of impact, though 900 foot-pounds is acceptable if bullet placement is precise. Loads that produce 1,500 foot-pounds at impact are optimum.

Ample energy must be accompanied by good bullet performance. A bullet is designed to incapacitate game by expending its energy inside the animal's body through expansion. Bullets

Comparative Ballistics for
Three Types of Whitetail Loads

	.30-30 Win. 170-Grain Power Point Winchester	.243 Win. 100-Grain Pointed Soft Point Remington	.30-06 Springfield 165-Grain Boattail Soft Point Federal Premium
Energy (Foot-pounds)			
100 yards	1,356	1,616	2,489
200 yards	990	1,332	2,146
300 yards	720	1,090	1,842
Trajectory (Drop in inches from muzzle)			
100 yards	3.9	2.1	2.3
200 yards	17.6	9.0	9.8
300 yards	44.5	21.7	23.1
Wind Drift (Inches of bullet drift in a 15-mph crosswind)			
100 yards	2.7	1.2	1.0
200 yards	11.8	5.3	4.2
300 yards	28.6	12.5	9.9
Necessary Lead (Lead in feet for a target crossing at 20 mph)			
50 yards	2.0	1.5	1.5
100 yards	4.3	3.1	3.3
200 yards	9.3	6.5	6.8
Uphill/Downhill Shooting (Inches bullet strikes high when shooting at a 45-degree angle, as opposed to level shooting)			
100 yards	1.2	.06	.07
200 yards	5.2	2.7	2.9
300 yards	13.1	6.4	6.8

Ballistics vary greatly among the various types of rifles suitable for whitetail hunting. Determine your needs, study ballistics tables, and try out some guns before selecting your rifle.

Photo by Mike Strandlund

Medium- to large-bore, high-velocity rifles like the .270, .308, and .30-06 are the most popular among whitetail hunters today.

Photo by Mike Strandlund

that drive through a deer's body without much expansion waste much of their energy. But a bullet that expands completely and stops within the deer delivers all its energy to the deer, causing the shock that downs deer immediately.

Centerfire deer rifles can be classified into three types according to these ballistic properties. They include large-bore, high-velocity loads; large-bore, low-velocity loads; and small-bore, high-velocity loads. The differences between loads within these categories are usually insignificant for practical purposes.

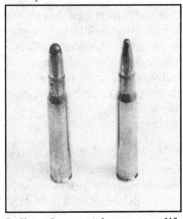

Bullet shape makes more difference than most hunters realize. The round-nose bullet on left has the most dependable expansion at shorter ranges. The better aerodynamics of the pointed soft-point (right) provides more accuracy and energy for longer-range shooting.

Large Bore, High Velocity

For whitetails, loads of this class would include the .270 caliber and larger with muzzle velocities over 2,800 feet per second. Common cartridges are the .270 Win., 7mm Rem. Mag., .308 Win., .30-06 Springfield, and the .300 Win. Mag.

This is the most popular class of cartridge among whitetail

hunters today, and with good reason. They have good hunting accuracy, flat trajectory, and high energy. With a good scope and an excellent shooter behind it, most of these rifles are capable of taking whitetails at up to 350 yards. They are the most effective at any range. While any hunting loads in this category could be considered good whitetail ammo, bullet selection is important. Bullets should have a semi-jacketed, soft lead point—not a hollow point that expands too quickly, or a solid point, which will not expand at all. Pointed bullets, especially boattails, do not slow as soon as round-nosed bullets. This gives flatter trajectory and more energy at any range. At short shooting distances, there's not much difference. But at maximum range, a pointed bullet may have up to *twice* the energy of a rounded bullet in the same load. It will also drift only half as far in the wind, which could make the difference between a hit and a miss. Also, bullets that are heavier in relation to their diameter retain energy better than shorter, lighter bullets. The main advantage of round-nosed bullets is that they often expand the best at short range.

Some hunters might consider the magnum calibers too much for whitetails. Another perspective is that as long as the shot is well placed, an overabundance of energy will not ruin any more meat. And the more powerful calibers will kill, rather than cripple, some animals in case of accidentally poor bullet placement.

Large Bore, Low Velocity

Enduring from the days of blackpowder cartridges are several loads considered primitive by modern standards, but which nonetheless have accounted for more whitetails than almost any other. The venerable .30-30 Win., .300 Savage, .32 Special, .35 Rem., and .45-70 Government are among those still manufactured. These, and the modern .357 Mag. and .44 Mag., are slow-velocity, large-caliber rifle loads acceptable for short-range whitetail hunting.

Photo by Mike Strandlund

Lever-actions in calibers like .30-30 and .32 Special are pleasant to carry and shoot. However, their comparatively low energy, mediocre accuracy, and limited range make them unsuitable for use in many deer hunting situations.

While these are all traditional whitetail cartridges, most of them have dubious energy compared to higher-velocity loads. Using the 1,200 foot-pounds rule, loads like the .30-30 are good only out to 100 yards or so. Even the .444 Marlin, which starts with more energy than a .30-06 due to its mass, has only half the energy of that .30-06 at 200 yards. The bullet also drops twice as far.

The major problem with guns in this category is that once velocity falls below 2,000 feet per second or so, bullets fail to expand properly. If you have doubts about your caliber's energy, use the larger soft-point bullets with medium-weight jackets. While the larger bullets may start with less velocity and energy than a smaller bullet of the same design, the larger projectile will retain more energy and actually be traveling faster than the smaller bullet at hunting ranges in most cases. The difference in trajectory is negligible.

There's a long-standing belief among deer hunters that slower, heavier, round-nosed bullets of strong build break through brush and remain intact better than lighter bullets. This may be true in comparing a 50-grain hollowpoint to a 250-grain hard-nose, but there is very little difference in brush-bucking ability among the more common bullet weights of 130 to 180 grains. All of them will tumble and fly erratically when they strike obstructions. The way to deal with an obstruction is to shoot around it — not through it with a more sluggish bullet.

Small Bore, High Velocity

High-velocity loads of .27 caliber and less are successfully used by some whitetail hunters, especially people who hunt open country or who are sensitive to the heavier recoil of larger calibers.

Common cartridges include the .257 Roberts, .25-06 Rem., 6mm Rem., and the .243 Win. Shooting bullets of 90 to 120 grains, these loads offer very flat trajectory, superb accuracy, good bullet expansion, and ample energy at ranges under 200 yards. The ultra-high-velocity .22 calibers may be acceptable in some cases, though they are outlawed for whitetail hunting in many areas. Loads like the .220 Swift and .22-250 Rem. have about 1,200 foot-pounds at 100 yards. But they are designed for varmints, not deer, and should not be used for whitetail hunting.

Rifle Actions and Models

Most deer hunters put as much thought into selecting their rifle's action and model as in the type of cartridge they shoot. They know the model has a bearing on cost, accuracy, dependability, speed of firing, and caliber available. It also determines their rifle's character — the feeling a hunter has for his rifle and its operation, which adds to the enjoyment of hunting.

Deer hunters have several action types to choose from: bolt-action, lever-action, pump, semi-automatic, single-shot, and others. Each action type has slight variations depending on manufacturer and model, and each has benefits and drawbacks as a whitetail rifle.

Bolt-Action

The bolt-action has become the most popular whitetail rifle. Chambered in virtually all deer-hunting calibers, it is renowned as the most dependable and accurate of all types. It is available in very inexpensive military surplus and sporting makes or fancy, high-priced custom models. The bolt-action is easy to maintain and is hardier than most other types. Its main disadvantage is that it is slow to operate for most hunters — which is academic with a well-placed first shot.

Lever-Action

Steeped in hunting tradition, the lever-action is popular among hunters who like its compactness and heritage. Lever-actions have historically been chambered for slow loads with rounded bullets. The tubular magazine does not accommodate pointed bullets, which could detonate the primer in the next cartridge. Some lever-actions are manufactured with box or rotary magazines and chambered for loads like the .308.

The lever-action is not known for outstanding accuracy, but it is satisfactory for the short ranges of most of its loads. Lever-actions are fairly dependable, but models with exposed hammers are not as safe as those with conventional safety catches. Some models are difficult or impossible to fit with a standard scope. Most lever-action rifles are comparatively inexpensive.

Pump-Action

The pump or slide-action rifle is growing in popularity among hunters as a good compromise deer gun. It has the load selection and dependability of the bolt-action and operating speed of the lever gun. Its action is actually faster to cycle than a lever, and the forward/backward movement does not pull the sights away from the target. The main drawback of a pump gun is that the fore-end may rattle and alert a nearby deer. Slide-action rifles are medium-priced.

Semi-Automatic

Like the pump, semi-autos have less accuracy than full-stock bolt-actions. But for most practical hunting purposes, the difference is insignificant. The semi-auto's obvious advantage is that it allows very quick follow-up shots. It also absorbs much recoil, which is more comfortable for the shooter. A common criticism of the autoloader is its comparative lack of dependability. But a well-maintained semi-auto, even in poor weather, seldom malfunctions. This action is not allowed for deer hunting in all states, however. Semi-autos are in about the same price range as pumps.

Single-Shots and Double-Barrels

Today's rarest deer rifles, single-shots are relegated to shooting purists who believe deer should be taken with a single, sure shot. Single-shots are generally among the most accurate and dependable of all rifles. Most guns in this category are of very high quality and expensive. Single-shots have either a falling-block or hinge action. Other hinge-action rifles include double-barrels and drillings (three-barreled guns). There are no American manufacturers of the latter models, and their use for whitetail hunting is negligible.

Shotguns for Deer

Stray bullets from high-power rifles can be dangerous in urbanized areas where there are large numbers of deer hunters. Deer hunters may be required to use shotgun slugs or buckshot, which lose energy in a much shorter range than rifle bullets.

Slugs and Buckshot

Shotgun slugs are a solid lead alloy weighing as much as an ounce and a half. They shoot straight from the smoothbores because the slugs themselves are rifled with deep grooves. Buckshot suitable for whitetails includes 000, 00, and 0 sizes (.36, .33, and .32 caliber) with pellet counts of between eight and 12 in 2¾ 12-gauge loads. Each normally shoots best through a modified or improved-cylinder choke.

Slugs do not have the tremendous short-range energy that many hunters believe. At 50 yards, a 12-gauge slug has about the same energy as a .30-30, and at 75 yards it falls below the 1,200-foot-pounds minimum. Slugs are also comparatively inaccurate, though adequately straight-shooting for these short

Photos by Mike Strandlund

Shotgun slugs are very effective short-range whitetail loads, but beads and barrel ribs make very poor slug sights. Use a scope, electronic sight, or slug barrel with iron sights.

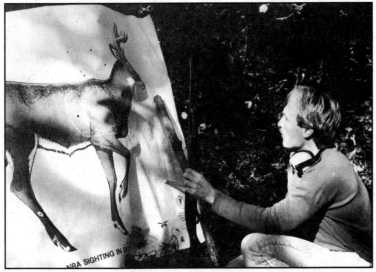

Buckshot is very limited in its usefulness for deer hunting. Make sure to test your gun, load, and effective range before hunting.

ranges. The sure range of buckshot is even more restricted—35 yards is about tops depending on gun, load, and conditions.

Despite the drawbacks of shotguns, many hunters prefer them for the type of hunting they do. A shotgun slug will break through light brush that would sidetrack a bullet; buckshot will find openings. Buckshot also makes you more likely to hit a close-running deer.

Shotgun Characteristics

Just about any shotgun is suitable for deer hunting, though some are far superior to others. The main problem is a sighting system—a shotgun bead is not conducive to accurate slug placement. Many hunters buy a barrel designed for slug shooting with front and rear iron sights. Others purchase a scope and mount, which is available for some models. Double-barrel shotguns are inferior to pump and semi-auto models in suitability for deer hunting. Each barrel of a double is likely to have its own point of impact. Autoloaders are a good choice because they offer quicker follow-up shots and ease the harsh recoil of a slug load.

Muzzleloaders

One of the fastest-growing outdoor sports, muzzleloading is

popular among whitetail hunters. Most muzzleloading whitetail hunters also use a modern firearm, hunting with a "frontstuffer" to take advantage of an extra hunting season and to explore the ways of pioneer hunters.

Blackpowder hunting is a whole different game from hunting with modern firearms—there are more considerations for gun handling, shooting, safety, and hunting techniques. There are infinite combinations of guns and loads.

States commonly require a minimum of .45 caliber for deer hunting, though the bullet's retained energy is largely determined by the powder charge and type of projectile used. A .45-caliber rifle with 60 grains of powder and a patched ball has only about 700 foot-pounds at 50 yards. Energy is increased with more powder, a larger or more streamlined bullet, a bigger bore, and a longer barrel. To reach the 1,200 foot-pounds level at 50 yards, you need a .50-caliber with 90 grains of powder and a conical bullet.

Among the choices available to a muzzleloading hunter are flintlock or percussion ignition; short-barreled half-stock rifles or long-barreled full-stock guns; black powder or Pyrodex pro-

NRA *Staff Photo*

One of the fastest-growing shooting sports, hunting with a muzzleloader is a satisfying, challenging way to take a whitetail.

Well-practiced handgunners with high-quality equipment can take whitetails. Only magnum-class handguns should be considered for deer hunting.

pellent; and round ball or conical projectiles. Shooters must make sure they match their calibers to their propellants (coarser grain for larger bores) and their projectiles to their bore (slow twist for balls, fast twist for bullets). Some guns are much easier to maintain and have more accurate sights than others. In short, a muzzleloader/hunter must be thoroughly familiar with both sports before pulling a trigger or taking to the woods.

Handguns

Even newer than the 20-year-old muzzleloading rage is the widespread interest in handgun hunting. Many states have recently legalized handguns for whitetail hunting.

A glance at ballistics tables will quickly reveal that handgun ammo has much less energy than traditional deer loads. Even the .44 Magnum has less than 800 foot-pounds at 50 yards from a revolver. A .357 Magnum, with only around 500 foot-pounds at the muzzle, should not be used for whitetail hunting.

This requires very exact bullet placement — another problem for the handgun hunter. Most first-time handgunners are amazed at how *poorly* they shoot a handgun with open sights.

A way around both problems is to use a scoped single-shot pistol rather than a revolver. Scoped pistols can nearly equal the accuracy of scoped rifles. With no cylinder/barrel gap to let gas pressure escape, a pistol generates considerably more bullet energy. There is also a wider selection of calibers in single-shot pistols.

Because of their low velocity, bullets should have semi-jacketed hollowpoints to promote expansion.

Sights and Scopes

Your deer gun is only as good as its sights. Iron sights may limit your range to 75 yards or so; installation of a good scope could extend it to over 300.

A scope can improve a shooter's performance immensely. There are many types of scopes, each with optics of varying quality, and with different features for different purposes. An open-country hunter might prefer the precision of a fixed-magnification scope with high power — perhaps 6x. In thick cover, low magnification is better — 1.5x, 2x, or 4x. Most whitetail hunters prefer variable-power units. Scopes of about 1.5x–4x or 2x–7x are most popular.

Firearm Accessories

A few pieces of equipment are essential for the firearms hunter. A good case is a must for traveling — a hard case is much more protective than the soft type. If you use a scope, you should have quick-detachable scope covers to keep moisture off the lenses. Many hunters use slings to ease the weight of the gun and as a shooting aid. An even better shooting aid is a pair of shooting sticks — a couple of yard-long dowels loosely attached three inches from the top make a good gun rest that can greatly improve accuracy.

Bowhunting Equipment

While bowhunting is the toughest way to pursue the whitetail, archers have refined their sport in recent years. The numbers of deer taken and the hunter success rate have both increased dramatically with improvements in equipment, hunter skills, and increased deer populations. In Wisconsin, for example, 40 hunters took one deer in the 1934 bowhunting season—the nation's first. By 1950 there were 12,000–15,000 bowhunters, but still they killed only 383 deer. In 1970 bowhunter success was up to 6½ percent with 101,573 bowhunters taking 6,520 deer. Hunter success rose steadily and 10 years later 155,386 bowmen took 20,954 deer for a success rate of 13½ percent. The trend continues — most recent figures show that in 1986, success reached 19 percent with 216,186 hunters taking 40,490 whitetails.

Today, over 2 million bowhunters spend $180 million annually on bowhunting equipment. Bowhunting was revolutionized with the advent of compound bows and related equipment. While the compound was invented in the 1930s, it wasn't until about 1970 that manufacturers and promoters brought together large numbers of compound bows and the archers interested in them. With the more efficient bows, sights, and accessories, many archers could achieve better accuracy much sooner than when shooting recurves or longbows without sights. The equipment has become even more refined in the last 20 years.

Bows for Whitetails

Compound bows have become by far the most popular style of bow used by big game hunters. Still, many hunters cling to traditional recurves and longbows, and there is a strong trend in the return to these "stick bows." Each type of bow has advantages and disadvantages for the whitetail hunter.

Compound Bows

The compound bow uses a pulley/cable system to let the archer shoot a heavier bow and to decrease the bow's draw weight as the shooter approaches full draw. There are many designs; early compounds used four pulleys—one at each limb end and two near the handle. Now most compounds have pulleys only at the limb ends, but there are many innovative designs, built mainly for increased arrow speed or greater let-off at full draw. High arrow velocity and let-off are the main features of the compound bow. These attributes combine to let an archer shoot arrows with a flatter trajectory, which increases accuracy.

Most compound bow shooters use pin sights—pins mounted at various heights just over the positioned arrow shaft. Each pin is set for a certain yardage—the shooter simply estimates yardage of the target and keeps the pin set for that yardage on target as he shoots. The pin may be aligned with the string or with

Photo by Mike Strandlund

With better equipment and accumulated knowledge of hunting white-tails, bowhunters have increased their deer hunting success greatly in recent years.

a peep sight installed on the string. There are many other types of bow sights, also.

The flat arrow flight, a sighting system, and accessories like stabilizers and mechanical releases help most archers achieve their best accuracy with a compound bow. But these bows are not always best in hunting situations. They are slower to draw, make more noise, and are not as reliable as bare bows. With sights, the hunter must estimate the distance — often in just a second or two. For this reason, some bowhunters believe instinctive shooting with a recurve or longbow is best for deer hunting.

Longbows and Recurves

Some compound shooters scoff at these "antiques," but the fact remains: In man's history as a hunter, he has taken more deer with longbows and recurves than any other type of hunting tool.

The straight-limbed longbow relies on its long limbs for well-balanced storage and release of energy. The double flex of a recurve bow operates something like two separate energy sources, so its limbs may be shorter. In both bows, the most important thing is an even cast — limbs must be of equal strength, and the draw weight must increase gradually, rather than "stacking" near full draw. Some shooters believe they can shoot longbows more accurately while others prefer recurves. A few archers put sights on these bows, but most shoot either instinctively, by changing their anchor point, or by estimating where to hold the arrow tip in relation to the target.

These bows can be very effective in the hands of practiced archers. The key word here is *practiced* — it takes long and regular shooting with a stick bow to achieve and maintain good accuracy.

Arrows and Accessories

Aluminum is the dominant arrow shaft material on the market today, with graphite, cedar, and other materials preferred by a few archers. Shafts must have correct flexibility matched to your particular bow's weight and draw length.

Very important are the type of broadhead and fletching you use on your arrow. A broadhead must be razor sharp to ensure it gets maximum penetration and cuts rather than pushes blood vessels aside. Most bows shoot most consistently with a certain type of broadhead — try several to find the best. The best feather fletching or plastic vanes also depend on the type of bow and arrow you use. Stick bows with heavy arrows need the most substantial arrow stabilizer.

Other bowhunting accessories include a quiver, sights, bow stabilizer, string silencers, brush buttons, shooting tab, glove, or mechanical release, and other shooting and sighting aids. Some hunters use a string tracker—several hundred yards of light, strong string attached to their arrow and bow, which helps them recover wounded game. If you use such a device, practice shooting with it first to see if it affects your arrow flight.

CHAPTER 4

DEER HUNTING MARKSMANSHIP

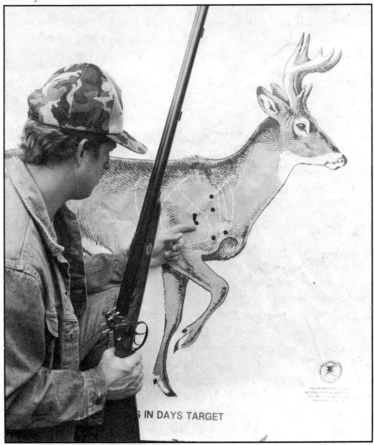

Even more important than the gun you use is an ability to use it well. Hunters have a responsibility to the game and to themselves to become good marksmen and shoot only within their effective range.

I n poor parts of Old Mexico, farmers feed their families white-tail venison secured with a .22 rimfire. At the same time too many of their northern neighbors, unprepared and over-confident, miss their deer with a fancy, high-power rifle they half expect to shoot by itself.

While the Mexican is certainly undergunned, he illustrates a principal point: More important than the firearm is the hunter behind it. It is desire to become as skilled as possible with a gun, and dedication to use it responsibly, that separates a true hunter from the weekend warriors.

Before he ever takes to the woods, the whitetail hunter must have an understanding with his gun or bow. He must know where it shoots, and that it will do so consistently. He must be intimately familiar with its workings and well-practiced with its shooting. And he must have a firm idea of where to aim and when — and when not — to pull the trigger.

Sighting-In Rifles

Sighting-in a rifle consists of holding your gun rock-solid as you shoot targets with hunting loads, adjusting sights or scope be-tween shots until bullets strike consistently at your point of aim.

A bench rest or similar rest is mandatory at this step. Don't make the mistake of trying to sight-in from an unsteady posi-tion. Save the sitting, standing, and prone shooting for practice *after* your gun is on target.

Benchrest Procedure

Proper benchrest shooting requires careful technique. Start with a solid bench that won't wobble when you lean into it and a solid seat at a height that affords comfortable shooting. Rest the rifle's fore-end (not the barrel) on sandbags, and place another sand-bag under the buttstock. Adjust the sandbags so the sights are on target with the rifle well seated in the sandbags. Test the rifle's forward/backward movement for smoothness, so the recoiling gun would not be thrown to one side because of uneven pressure or catching sling swivels.

Set up the target about two feet off the ground against a high earthen backstop. The best type of target depends on the rifle and sights you use; a small bullseye, perhaps with crossed lines you can align with your crosshairs, is best if you use a scope. A bigger bullseye, maybe three inches across, is better for open sights. A spotting scope is handy for checking hits.

Photo by Mike Strandlund

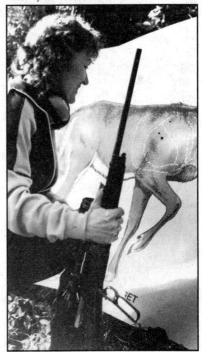

Develop good benchrest technique for testing accuracy of your gun and loads. After you're sighted-in, practice with realistic hunting conditions and shooting positions.

Sighting-In Distance

There are several variables that determine the best sighting-in distance. With a new gun or newly installed scope, start close with a large target for coarse sight adjustments. Then move the target back to the range at which you expect to encounter game. Because of the thick cover they inhabit, most whitetails are shot at a range of 35 to 50 yards. But longer shots are common in some areas.

If you expect the closer-range shooting, sight-in at 75 yards. Any rifle zeroed at this range will shoot well within the vital zone of a deer between point-blank and at least 125 yards—about maximum for muzzleloaders, shotguns, handguns, and rifles in the .30-30 class.

Long-range rifles zeroed at 200 yards will shoot a maximum of about 2½ inches high at shorter ranges and 2½ inches low at 250–300 yards—both acceptable deviations for a hunter aiming at the center of a deer's shoulder. With most high-power calibers, you can zero your rifle at 25 yards. The bullet will be about two inches high at 100 yards, back on zero at about 200–250 yards, and a couple inches low at 300. Check trajectory tables for your particular cartridge to determine bullet impact at various ranges.

You can also use ballistics information to make sighting-in easier. For example, you may want to zero your .30-06 180-grain Remington pointed soft-point cartridge at 200 yards, but have only a 100-yard shooting range available. Simply adjust your sights until the bullets group 2½ inches high at 100 yards. They will be on target at 200 yards.

Adjusting to Point of Aim

For best results, be well-prepared before sighting-in your gun. With the target set against a safe backstop, check the rifle to ensure it is mechanically sound and the bore is clear. Pay particular attention that the sights or scope is secure and all action and sight screws are tight. Make initial sight adjustments with a bore-sighter, if you have one. With a bolt-action rifle, you may remove the bolt, view down the bore to the bullseye, secure the gun in that position, and adjust the sights to the target.

Wearing eye and ear protection, load your first round and make final adjustments to make sure your sights are on target. Take a firm, natural hold with the buttstock firm against your shoulder, and fire.

Shoot a three-shot group, and adjust your sights to get your next shot closer to the aiming point. With open sights, move the rear sight in the direction you want the next bullet to go (move it left if you want the bullet to go left, up if you want the bullet to strike higher). With a scope, turn the adjusting knobs the direction and amount indicated on the settings. Usually, the knobs are turned clockwise to move impact down or to the left, counterclockwise to move it up or to the right, and each click usually equals a quarter-inch or half-inch at 100 yards.

Once you're on target, shoot three-shot groups, adjusting between each, to fine-tune your zero. Then set your rifle aside for about a half-hour to let the barrel cool, clean the bore, and wipe it dry. Fire one careful shot. Let the barrel cool again, and fire a couple of times through the fouled bore. If impact changes significantly under these varying barrel conditions, be sure to match the final sight adjustment to the condition your rifle will be in when you take it hunting.

Zeroing Other Firearms

Slug shotguns, handguns, and muzzleloaders are sighted-in basically the same as rifles. With handguns, rest the gun butt and triggerguard on sandbags, being sure the barrel does not

Photo by Phil Johnston

The sights of handguns, muzzleloaders, and slug shotguns should be carefully adjusted according to expected shooting ranges. The trajectory of their projectiles changes point of impact considerably at varying yardages.

rest, which will cause the gun to shoot high. Hold it consistently with the two-handed grip you would use in a hunting situation. With a revolver, shoot through all the cylinders and watch for bullets shooting differently from certain cylinders. If you're using open sights, pick a small spot on your target, align the top of the front sight with the top of the rear sight, and center the front sight on the bottom of that spot. This gives you an unobstructed view beneficial when shooting at game. When aiming the handgun, focus on the sights; the target will have to appear somewhat out of focus.

When sighting-in a muzzleloader, be sure the entire loading procedure from powder measuring to ball tamping is consistent. Clean the bore between each shot. Fixed sights must be adjusted with a file; be sure not to file too much. You may change your sight picture instead, with a "fine bead" for close shots and more of the front sight visible for longer shots.

For the buckshot shooter, pattern testing is crucial. Try different loads, through different chokes, at different ranges until you find the best combination. Using a lifesize deer target, pattern loads at increasing distance until you can no longer keep at least two pellets in the vital zone of a deer; that's when you've surpassed the effective range of your gun and load.

Firearms Practice

Once your gun is sighted-in, the job is partly done. Now it's time to practice from hunting positions until you can place bullets consistently in a deer-sized vital area at the ranges you intend to shoot. The amount of practice you'll have to do depends on your shooting experience and the skill you want to achieve. Your practice will determine the range and the conditions under which you can responsibly shoot at deer.

The best way to practice is with a lifesize target such as NRA's Sighting-In Days deer target. You may also use a target with about a six-inch

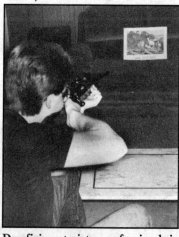

Photo by Mike Strandlund

Dry-firing at pictures of animals is good practice, allowing you to spend extra time working on hold, breath control, trigger-pull, and follow-through.

circle, six-inch paper plates, or other such targets that represent the approximate size of the lung/heart area of a whitetail.

Shoot from various positions at increasing ranges until you find your maximum effective range. You will also find that you can increase your range with practice. The less experienced you are, the more you can improve with practice.

Archery Sighting and Practice

If you're a new archer, read up on equipment tuning and shooting techniques. Archers need more study and practice than firearms shooters to successfully take whitetails.

If you shoot a compound bow, you will probably equip it with pin sights. With your bow well tuned and arrows matched to your draw weight and length, practice from about 10 yards until you develop a consistent anchor point, hold, and release. Then step off distances and adjust a pin to be on target at each distance you've selected. (Move pins down for a higher arrow impact, left to move impact right, and vice versa.)

Remember that point of impact will be different if you are on the ground or in a tree stand, if you change from field points to broadheads, if you wear light or bulky clothes, and under many other circumstances. Match your practice sessions as closely as possible to actual hunting situations. If you plan to hunt primarily from tree stands, practice primarily from elevated positions.

Photo by Mike Strandlund

Frequent, high-quality practice is the key to taking a whitetail with archery equipment.

Improving estimation of distance is one of the most important elements of practice for the sight-shooting archer. Rather than shooting at certain yardages, practice with targets at unknown range. For the instinctive archer, shooting without sights, daily practice at various targets is the key.

Quality Practice

Most hunters realize that the vital area of a deer is usually harder to hit than a target of the same size. But too few hunters prepare mentally and physically for that challenge.

Movement, obstructions, severe angles, and excitement are a few of the factors that hurt hunting accuracy. Some are con-

Photo by Mike Strandlund

If you hunt with a handgun, practice under actual hunting conditions until you determine your effective range, keeping in mind the energy limitations of your gun.

trollable; some are not. But *quality* shooting practice can minimize all these deterrents. As you target shoot, imagine that you are in a real hunting situation. This technique, called visualization, is used by competitive shooters and other athletes to simulate the real thing. It helps you rehearse mentally as well as physically. It's a great aid in preventing overexcitement when you encounter the deer you want. If you visualize correctly, you can feel the pressure of a close encounter with a deer each time you take a practice shot. When you reach your hunt's climax, you feel as if you've been through it a thousand times, and you suffer much less stress.

Visualizing also helps you

Photo by Bill Bynum

The best hunting marksmen are those who visualize actual situations as they practice, so they are ready for any circumstance that might arise in the field.

deal with tough shooting situations in the deer woods. While practicing, imagine the scenarios you might encounter. Would you shoot at a deer walking through thick trees, or wait until he—hopefully—stopped? Where would you aim? Would you shoot at all at a running deer? Would you swing, lead, and shoot or would you hold on an opening and fire just as he arrived? How far do you lead a deer? You should have these questions answered before the hunt to avoid the indecisiveness that could cost you a deer.

Where to Aim

Bullet placement on deer is important for several reasons. A quick kill is humane and ensures you'll recover the animal. The meat will be in better condition if you can avoid shooting large muscles and digestive organs, cause the deer as little stress as possible, and recover the animal immediately.

In hunting situations, deer are killed by blood loss, destruction of vital organs, or disruption of the nervous system (brain/spinal cord). An unalert deer may be downed immediately by the shock of a high-energy bullet, while adrenaline may keep a pursued deer going after multiple hits.

In nearly every case, the best place to aim is the chest area containing the heart and lungs. This is by far the largest vital zone on a whitetail. It is surrounded by other vital areas — the neck, backbone, and liver — so a slightly errant shot will still get the job done.

Viewed from the side, the heart/lung area extends from the front of the shoulder to almost midbody. A shot at the point of the "elbow" destroys the heart, while a shot to the front of the shoulder may penetrate lungs and break leg bones, which will usually drop the deer immediately. Both of these shots ruin meat, however. A shot behind the shoulder, halfway between the back and belly, will break through the ribcage and penetrate the lungs, destroying no meat. Archers should note and avoid shooting toward the front-leg bone, which will stop an arrow before it can reach vitals.

A shot in or very near the spinal cord or brain will drop the deer instantly. But these are very risky shots. The brain is small and the spine is narrow. Most backbone shots are inadvertent — lung shots that have gone high. They do not kill immediately, and another shot will be necessary.

A bullet that breaks a neck bone will kill instantly, but there are certain risks with neck shots. A deer can move its neck more suddenly than its chest area. If the shot strikes the neck but does not break the spinal cord, it may hit a major blood vessel and cause quick death. But occasionally a bullet may pass through a deer's neck without killing effect.

The liver and large arteries are also vital areas, but are seldom good targets. The liver is much smaller than lungs and lies dangerously close to the stomach and intestines. Arteries are also too small to aim for in most cases, and are mostly imbedded in muscle.

Shooting Whitetails

In a sense, the purpose of hunting is simply to put yourself in a position for a quick, humane kill. You may have your deer spotted, but you have to keep hunting until you get the right shot. When to shoot, as well as where and how, depend on your firearm or bow and the situation.

Many gun hunters are reluctant to take a going-away shot. But at closer ranges, rifles of the .270 class and up can penetrate

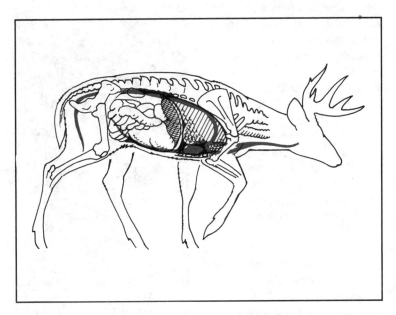

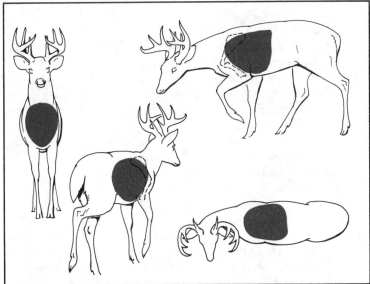

These diagrams show the relative positioning of a whitetail's vital organs and how the vital zone appears to the hunter at various shooting angles. In the top drawing, the heart can be seen just above the elbow, and the lungs, liver and major arteries are shown in color. The bottom picture shows this shaded zone from head-on, quartering away, broadside, and from above. Note how the shoulder blade and upper leg bones shield the vital zone at different angles.

79

the length of a deer's body and reach the vitals from behind. For straight-on shots, hold well up on the throat; aiming for the "chest" may only catch the brisket—a nonvital combination of hair and bone.

Each shooting situation is unique, often requiring fast thinking and good judgment on a fleeting opportunity. Here are three common scenarios and ideas on handling them:

Photo by Stan Warren

- Deer strolling laterally at close-to-medium range. Immediately determine whether you have a few seconds to shoot or must shoot immediately. The animal may soon disappear below a rise or behind cover. If so, take

There is seldom an excuse for shooting without a gun rest in hunting situations. Make sure there is always a gun rest at your stand. When still-hunting, pause near trees that you could use for support if a shot should arise.

the steadiest rest available and shoot. If you have some time to prepare, get a steady rest, put the sights on the deer, and observe its behavior. Will it get closer? Strolling deer usually stop every few steps. Wait till it's still, and scan the path between you and the deer for bullet or arrow obstructions. Try to wait until the deer's head is obscured or it is looking directly away before you ease slowly into shooting position. Be careful that there are no other deer with the one you plan to shoot that could see you move and sound the alarm.

- Deer hurrying or running laterally at midrange. In cover, this is the shot that causes the most anxiety for hunters — especially if the deer is bounding. If you lead and swing with the deer, there's a good chance your bullet may hit an obstruction. If you hold on an opening and time your shot, lead is more critical and vertical accuracy is less precise. In woods, you usually have a better than even chance of hitting an obstruction if you simply lead the deer; it's usually better to hold on an opening. Good judgment, knowledge of necessary lead, and experience with shooting at moving targets are the best solutions to this problem.

Photo by Ernest Alfstad, U.S. Fish and Wildlife Service

Photo by Pierre Bernier, Government of Quebec

Whitetails can present very difficult shots, especially when you're still-hunting or putting on a drive. When the deer are bounding or partially obscured by brush, it's usually best to wait for a better shot.

• Deer standing at long range. In open country and rolling, clean woods, long shots on whitetails are common. It is necessary to consider factors like trajectory, wind drift, and up/down angle adjustment when shooting 150 yards or more.

On long shots, you may have to hold several inches higher than your target. But if the deer is considerably higher or lower than you are, the angle may negate the trajectory— you may have to hold right on, or even a bit under the target. Wind drift affects long-range shots more than most hunters realize. (See table on page 54.)

Maximizing Hunting Accuracy

While hunters spend hundreds of dollars and hundreds of hours getting the best accuracy out of their guns and ammo, there are some shortcuts that many overlook.

The best way you can improve your hunting accuracy is to make sure you have a gun rest. There is seldom an excuse for shooting offhand at a deer. Sitting, with elbows locked inside your knees, is better. But in most cases you should be able to use a solid rest. When you walk and pause during still-hunting, always stop next to a small tree you could use as a rest if a deer appeared. Stand hunters should always have a rest built into their blind or tree stand.

A shooting-sticks bipod is a great aid in hunting. There are commercial models available, or you can make your own. Simply tie two three-foot dowels together three inches from one end. Twist them so that the long ends open to provide a wide, steady support and the tops form a crotch to rest your rifle's fore-end. The increase in accuracy is considerable.

Archers, too, should experiment with equipment to find their best accuracy. Things like the string's nocking point and the arrow spine, fletching, and broadhead have great effects on accuracy.

Here are some more tips on improving hunting accuracy:

• Accurize your rifle. You can get significantly more accuracy from a rifle by glass-bedding the barrel, adjusting the trigger, and other improvements.

• Refine your shooting techniques. This includes finding your most accurate position, breath control, hold control, trigger control, and follow-through. Work on breaking bad habits like flinching or pressing the trigger when the sight picture isn't perfect.

- Keep your gun clean and in good condition. Use a good solvent and brush to remove lead or copper build-up in the bore.
- Practice under realistic shooting conditions. Shoot from different positions in the woods while wearing your hunting clothes. Learn how to work your rifle's action quickly.
- When you can't practice with live ammo, practice through dry-firing. Pull the trigger on photos of deer in your living room. Concentrate on good technique and, for obvious reasons, take special care that your gun is unloaded.
- For more information on rifles and shooting, refer to the NRA publication *The Basics of Rifle Shooting.*

Photo by Tom Tabor

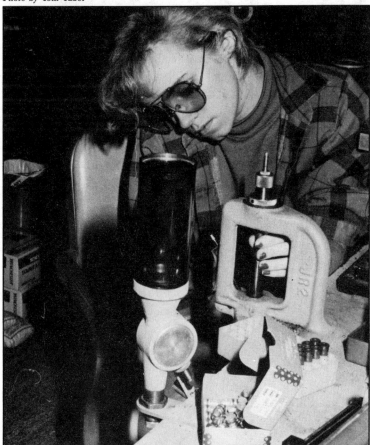

Most hunters can improve their firearm's accuracy by reloading their own ammo.

CHAPTER 5

SCOUTING AND
HUNT PREPARATION

H e's the fastest thing in his neck of the woods. But he normally doesn't need to be. Always alert, he'll see or smell or hear you before he needs to run. He'll catch your scent a cornfield away. He'll see you scratch your nose well out of rifle range. He'll hear your safety click and be gone before

Photo by Wade Bourne

Dedicated scouting is the key to getting a sure shot on a trophy whitetail buck.

you can shoot. He'll let you walk past, then sneak away as invisibly as a black cat at midnight. Sometimes, he won't *get out* of bed till you've *gone* to bed.

He's the whitetail deer. He knows this hunting game far better than you do, and he always has the home field advantage. If you want to genuinely challenge him to this contest, rather than hoping to win by luck, you've got to come up with a game plan.

Year-Round Deer Hunting

The plan should start early. Two weekends before season isn't early enough for a committed deer hunter. Neither is two months. Your planning and scouting for next season should begin during the previous deer season and continue through winter, spring, and summer.

Think of deer hunting as an ongoing affair rather than a series of individual seasons. If you didn't get your buck this year, you haven't failed; you just haven't succeeded yet. Chances are, you'll return to the same hunting area next season. What should you do differently? What did you learn this year about the hunting area, deer herd, or a particular buck? Make notes and maps if they help. Use your experiences to refine strategy for next year. If you have second thoughts about the place you've been hunting, you may want to try another area next year. Start looking early.

Photo by Mike Strandlund

Glassing field edges at evening is a good way to scope out the local deer herd before hunting starts.

Photo by Wade Bourne

One of the first steps in preparing for a deer hunt is gaining access to some prime hunting property. With a sincere approach, you may get permission to hunt land that is posted to other hunters.

Scouting with a Purpose and a Plan

Too many people prepare for deer season like this: They get some information, maybe a game department report, and find a place of high whitetail density within driving distance of home. Then a weekend or two before season, they drive to the area, saunter into the woods (not too far from the car, for fear of getting lost or tired) and throw together a makeshift blind near a deer trail. Some hunters don't even go this far; they just drive to the nearest public hunting area on opening morning and start walking around.

These hunters, with lots of luck, may get a buck. But they are seldom among those hunters who seem to beat the odds and bring home venison year after year. For consistent success, you need to know exactly what you're doing—and what deer are doing—when season arrives.

It is a myth that you have to go to an area of consistently high kills, or the country with the greatest density of deer, for the best chance of success. There are many other variables involved. Most important to realize is that a deer herd does not occupy a region or a county. It inhabits a "pocket" of only a couple hundred acres or less. It is very possible you could go to an area of moderate whitetail population and find a creekbottom, shelterbelt, or ridge saddle that has more deer traffic than a similar place in an area of higher deer density. *Scout coverts, not counties.*

You may have located some of these pockets with potential on previous trips to the woods and fields. If not, identify some general areas you'd like to hunt, maybe through talks with other hunters or wildlife managers. Then scout them thoroughly to isolate the better pockets. The more good, huntable pockets you have available the better — especially if you're hunting throughout a long season.

As you scout, keep in mind the type of deer hunting you'll do. If you are looking for a trophy buck, you're better off scouting

Photo by Len Rue Jr.

Carefully reading habitat and sign will indicate pockets of high whitetail density and the best location for a stand.

wilderness areas that have fewer hunters and fewer —but older— bucks. What constitutes a good place to hunt varies depending on whether you are still-hunting, stand hunting, or driving; hunting with a rifle, shotgun, or bow.

How to Scout

Whitetail scouting begins with looking at the big picture, then systematically narrowing it down to a certain patch of cover, or maybe a specific blind site. In a good whitetail woods you might see deer anywhere, but there are invariably certain spots that are definitely best. If you're in heavy cover, or hunting with a bow, your stand site must be exact—a few yards off, and that buck of a lifetime might get by you.

This means you must pay attention to details. There are several specifics to examine when scouting, including the following:

- **Escape Routes**
- **Hunter Movement**
- **Shed Antlers**
- **Deer Trails**
- **Bedding Areas**
- **Rubs and Scrapes**
- **Deer Movement Patterns**
- **Feeding and Watering Areas**
- **Terrain and Obstructions to Deer Travel**
- **Favorability for Certain Hunting Methods**

You can scout for some of these details any time of year. It's best to look for deer patterns, feeding areas, and hunter movements close to or during hunting season.

Plotting Escape Routes

Some of the most useful knowledge you will gain while hunting or scouting concerns escape routes. During firearms season in most areas, the great majority of deer are taken as they move to avoid another hunter. In escaping, deer may consciously follow a certain route. If you know where those routes are, you can put yourself in the best position to take a deer.

In some places it is impossible to predict where a deer will run when frightened. In others, it is quite easy. Deer tend to run toward thicker cover, take a path with good cover, and run uphill when they encounter hunters. Bucks prefer to sneak through cover, rather than make a break, if they can do so unseen. Deer that are very frightened try to cover lots of ground quickly; they tend to take the easiest routes.

In situations where deer have few options, logic tells you where they are most likely to go. Better yet, you or your hunting partners may actually jump deer and see where they run.

In heavily hunted areas, or during drives, you can be assured that deer will be forced to move. If you've jumped deer, observed them, and made notes, you'll know where they are likely to run next time someone flushes them out. A deer that escapes unharmed by taking a certain route will be convinced that it is a safe way to elude hunters. He will be encouraged to take the same path next time. Construct your stands accordingly.

Photo by Mike Strandlund

A stand near a deer's escape route may get you close to deer that are fleeing other hunters. These are the best stand locations in areas of high hunter density.

Hunter Movement

Another type of scouting you can do while hunting, and related to escape routes, is examining the area's hunter movement. Hunters nearly always move deer as they go to their deer stands in the morning, and again as they begin walking around a few hours later. In heavily hunted areas there may almost be a drive-line effect. For example, hunters typically line the scarce roads in public hunting areas the first few days of season, entering the woods after daylight. If you've accurately judged the effect of hunter movement, and set up on a deer escape route well before daylight, you are in a very good position to take a buck.

Immediately after the firearms season, do some thorough scouting to see where deer are bedding during the day. This will be their preferred haven, a place they feel safe when being hunted. Keep it in mind for next hunting season.

Conversely, you may want to avoid the effects of hunter movement. You may prefer to hunt deer in an undisturbed setting. If you're bowhunting, you need targets that are standing or slowly walking, rather than running or walking fast. If so, make note of places that seem to have fewer hunters. Local wildlife managers are glad to provide information about these areas—they prefer to distribute the pressure from hunters.

Postseason Head Count

Late in the hunting season, you jumped a good buck but didn't get him. Or maybe you heard of a real trophy that eluded another hunter. As far as you know, he wasn't taken, and you want to try for him next year. Is he still out there?

You may be able to find out. Soon after hunting seasons end, bucks begin dropping their antlers. Go on a late-winter search for these "pick-ups." Look for shed antlers between favorite bedding and feeding areas. If you find one, chances are the deer will be in the same place next year—with a bigger

Photo by Mike Strandlund

Finding "pick-ups," or shed antlers, is the best way of locating bucks that have survived the winter. Chances are the bucks will be around next hunting season, bigger than ever.

and better rack. Habitat loss, road kills, or winter die-off may wreck this plan, but odds are the deer will survive.

Trails and Bedding Areas

While looking for pick-ups, check other deer sign. Snow may reveal deer movement patterns that you could have overlooked if there wasn't snow during hunting season. After a fresh snowfall, find a single set of tracks and follow it. You may learn more about whitetails in one morning than you ever knew before.

Beds are especially easy to find in snow. Learn their locations in early winter, because it's likely these are the same beds deer use during late hunting season. Here's a valuable tip when examining bedding areas: Biologists have found that bucks usually urinate immediately after arising from their bed. Does usually walk away from their beds before urinating. If you find urine in a bed, it is likely the bed of a buck.

Photo Courtesy N.Y. Dept. of Environmental Conservation

Photo by Richard P. Smith

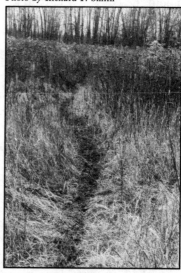

Deer trails may be obvious on wet or snow-covered ground, or in areas of especially high deer density. They are usually not this apparent; they may be indicated only by bent grass or indentations in forest ground litter.

Photo Courtesy Illinois Department of Conservation

Daytime deer beds can tell a careful scouter where to take a stand at first light. Look for beds located in cover; beds found in fields are usually made at night and are of little use to the hunter.

Rubs and Scrapes

Rubs and scrapes can yield valuable information during, after, or just before hunting season. A frequently used scrape is obviously among the best places to hunt during the rut. But scrapes and rubs also indicate preferred all-season travel and loafing areas of deer. The same scrapes and rubbing sites will likely be used by the same buck or a different buck the following fall. Scrapes may remain visible well into the spring and summer; you can study them year-round to establish patterns or to set up stands for your hunting the following fall.

Photos by Mike Strandlund

Tracks and droppings give a variety of information on the local deer — their numbers, size, travel patterns, and eating habits.

Photo by Mike Strandlund

Rubs also remain visible until the tree, typically killed by the girdling, topples over. Rubs, unless on well-used trails, are not necessarily good stand sites. But they can yield valuable information to the buck hunter. All bucks may rub on small trees, but rubs made on larger trees are made by larger bucks with larger racks. Thought by many hunters to be a fallacy, this phenomenon has been proven to be true by biologists.

Preseason feeding patterns

Rubs and scrapes are the buck hunter's vital signs. They can indicate the number, size, and habits of the area's antlered deer.

may or may not be similar to those of hunting season. It's imperative to monitor feeding habits close to hunting time — they may change weekly as different foods ripen and increased human movement in the woods causes deer to change their habits.

Spring and Summer Scouting

More deer hunting preparation can be done in spring and summer than many hunters realize. You have more spare time and can do more scouting without worry of disturbing deer close to hunting time. In early spring the woods are open, giving you

Photo by Mike Strandlund

Photo by Richard P. Smith

Whitetails are the least wary in late summer, often observed in fields and meadows in morning and late afternoon. This is a good time to scope the local deer herd and maybe pick the buck you want.

Photo Courtesy Wisconsin DNR

Spotlighting is the surest way to see deer and find their current evening feeding areas. Most areas have strict legal regulations on spotlighting.

a clear picture of the terrain and features so you can analyze probable travel routes. You can scout at your own pace, minding the details that can point to that ultimate stand location. Since deer habits change with the seasons, go by your notes from last season and old trails used for fall feeding patterns, rather than by current sign, when selecting stand sites.

Deer are the least wary this time of year, and you can often observe them in fields at dawn and dusk. A spotting scope mounted on the window of your vehicle is a great aid here. In some areas, it is legal to watch deer at night with a spotlight as long as you don't have a gun or bow in possession. This is the easiest and surest way of locating superior bucks after their antlers have formed in summer. Make note of their favorite places to enter and leave fields. Take care not to disturb the deer—for their benefit and yours.

Preseason Patterning

As hunting season approaches, scouting should become more frequent and discreet. Spend as much time as you can monitoring the deer's changing movements, but be very careful not to disturb them. Most scouting should be done at midday, and observations should be made at long range.

Some of the surest signs of current deer use are fresh tracks and droppings. While novices seem to put undue emphasis on actually spotting deer, experienced scouters know that finding this sign is as good as seeing the deer that made it. The only problem is that there is no reliable way of telling if the tracks or droppings were made by a buck or doe unless you *do* see the deer make it.

This sign can give you many other clues to the resident deer herd, however. After you've done a lot of scouting, you'll be able to spot and read sign easier. You'll know by the amount of tracks and droppings present whether a particular area has a comparatively large or small deer population.

Scouting at this time of year is aimed at determining current movement patterns of deer. While you never know for sure how deer will move, you should be able to develop an idea of where they generally travel, and where the best stand locations are for the best chance of getting within shooting range.

These areas of heavy deer activity are usually one of six types of locations:

- **Bedding Areas**
- **Feeding Areas**
- **Watering Areas**
- **Normal Travel Lanes**
- **Escape Routes**
- **Breeding Areas**

Funnels and Short Supplies

What you are looking for is a funnel, or bottleneck, where deer concentrate at a certain restricted area at certain times. Funnels are found at the thing a whitetail needs that is in shortest supply, whether that may be food, water, cover, or something else.

Imagine, for example, that you are hunting a farm with a small soybean field surrounded by a pine plantation. Deer have an unlimited area for bedding, but only a small area of preferred food. The funnel is at the food source. Picture a large apple orchard bordered by pastures and a thick, narrow swamp. Here bedding sites are in shortest supply, and deer will concentrate at the swamp. In the big woods, full of food and cover, the best funnels may be at bottlenecks on whitetail travel routes. Look for major trails on the downstream side of beaver dams and the edges of impenetrable thornbush thickets. Likewise, mountain-deer funnels are often travel routes — usually a saddle in a steep ridge, or where deer go around a pond, rock slide, or deep gully. In arid areas, waterholes are obviously the shortest in supply and the logical gathering ground for game. During the rut, deer seek

Photo by J. H. Johns, New Zealand Forest Service

Find a "funnel" such as a favorite fence crossing just before hunting season, and you've found a prime stand location.

Four types of funnels where deer may concentrate on their travels include (A) creek crossings below beaver dams (B) the top or bottom of
steep, impenetrable gullies (C) brushy creekbottoms or fence lines
through fields and (D) rare water sources in arid areas.

social centers. Activity will be most concentrated at fresh scrape
lines.

Determine the most likely funnels in the area where you plan
to hunt, and scout them first. Make note of the comparable
amounts of deer sign you find at each. Follow the sign deer leave
at and between feeding, bedding, and watering locations. Soon

Photo by Mike Strandlund

Some whitetail hunters are successful in making their own deer funnels — in this case, a fake breeding scrape made with scent taken from whitetails during the rut.

a pattern will develop, and you can plan your hunting around that pattern.

Scouting for Stands

When you have discerned a pattern, start planning your stand sites. You must consider the comparative amounts of sign, the type of hunting you plan to do, the time of day you'll be hunting, and the hunting pressure.

Everything depends on the time of day deer are making their sign. Trails through fields are usually useless to hunters, because these are normally made at night. But a field *entrance* trail is good for evening hunts early in the season. The entrances to heavily used bedding areas are good for morning hunts if you can get there undetected — which is usually difficult. Archers usually hunt undisturbed deer — which may or may not increase their chances. For heavily hunted areas on opening day of gun season, the best stands are often along escape routes that lead to thick cover.

Photo by Mike Strandlund

Permanent tree stands should be constructed months before hunting starts so deer get used to them.

Scouting for a Still-Hunt

When deer hunters think of scouting, they think of finding a good stand. But most hunters do some still-hunting (quietly sneaking) during the course of the season. With thorough scouting, you can have a plan for each area you still-hunt.

Still-hunting, done right, is not just a leisurely walk in the woods. Deer live in this forest every minute of their lives, and are well-adapted. In comparison, you're just an awkward, ill-adapted visitor. Deer have learned how to use the wind, cover, trails, and terrain in this specific area. If you want to still-hunt them effectively, you must, too.

The best approach to still-hunting is to sneak upwind toward deer bedding areas during their resting hours of late morning and early afternoon. Dawn, dusk, and mid-day are times of deer activity, and your chances are better from a stand. Keep this in mind as you explore the area, visualizing how you would hunt. Good ideas will develop.

Still-hunters should go on a preseason reconnaissance mission to find good areas for walking quietly through thick woods. These may include a logging road, deer path, or dry, dusty creekbed.

In scouting, locate as many deer bedding areas as possible. Pay special attention to beds in high grass and other locations conducive to shooting at breaking bucks. Make a note of the prevailing wind at various times of day, as well as paths that offer noiseless walking. If you jump deer, watch where they run. They've escaped that way once, and will probably run the same way next time they're flushed.

Scouting for Drives

With the logistics involved in transporting and setting up a dozen or more hunters, scouting and planning is most important for deer driving. You've got to have hunting areas identified, stand sites picked, and transportation planned before you have a dozen eager hunters breathing down your neck.

Keep in mind the number of hunters you'll have; this will determine the size of area you can drive. Get permission to hunt as many of these patches of cover as you can. Hike them and make note of bedding areas, escape routes, thickets, and stand sites. Consider the best ways of conducting drives there. Finally, plot them on a map for each hunter so you can systematically hunt and travel with as little wasted time on the road as possible.

Along with scouting, deer hunting preparation includes getting to know your equipment and getting your body in shape.

Part II

How to Hunt Whitetail Deer

CHAPTER 6
STAND HUNTING FOR WHITETAILS

A choice stand conceals or elevates the hunter from view and offers a good command of multiple travel routes or other types of deer funnels.

A good deer stand is the edge we hunters need over the vastly superior senses of the whitetail. The ideal stand makes you invisible to the deer and keeps it from hearing you. Placed downwind or crosswind of a place deer are sure to travel, that stand puts you in a perfect position for a shot. And since deer do not generally know you are there, your shots are at a standing or slowly moving target.

This may make stand hunting sound like a pushover, but experienced whitetail hunters know there is no such thing in this sport. A successful stand-hunt for deer comes from an intimate knowledge of the animal and how the game is played, and from minding the small details that add up to success.

An Ideal Deer Stand

The perfect whitetail stand is among good sign, between a bedding and feeding area, and overlooks an escape route or a place where deer go when disturbed. That ideal stand has a field of

NRA Staff Photo

Stand hunting defeats the whitetail's senses while enhancing those of the hunter, providing best chances for success.

view equal to the range you can accurately shoot, is elevated, and faces into the wind. It has a gun rest and few obstructions to bullets, arrows, or eyesight. The stand helps hide you and keep you quiet. It is also somewhat sheltered, accessible in the dark, and a reasonable deer-drag from a place to park your vehicle. It is safe and comfortable.

A deer stand with all these qualities is a real treasure; most hunters compromise and take a stand that is missing some of these elements. But perfect stands do exist, and are found with thorough, conscientious scouting.

Perhaps the best advantage to finding that perfect stand is that it gives you confidence. This confidence is assuring and keeps the fun of anticipation in the hunt. It keeps you seated through the long hours after your fellow hunters have become restless and started moving about—which is the best time to be on stand.

Selecting Stand Sites

Foremost in stand selection is finding a place where you have the best possible chance of getting a shot at deer—preferably bucks or maybe a certain buck. In cover, special attention must be given to the exact positioning of the tree stand or blind; a few feet either way may make the difference in whether you get your deer.

As discussed previously, the best location is normally a funnel or bottleneck where deer concentrate during the times you plan to be on stand. These sites are in one of two places: They are among **routine** travel routes or destinations, usually trails running between bedding, feeding, and watering areas. Or they may be **evasion** routes, which whitetails take when alarmed by human activity.

The best routine routes speak for themselves through the deer sign that abounds there. These are usually the best stand locations for bowhunters, primitive-arms hunters, and opening-day gun hunters—in other words, for hunting deer that have not been spooked.

An intersection of trails used currently and frequently is a good stand site on routine routes. A narrow neck of dry land between dense, deep swamps is superb. So are the feeding, bedding, and watering sites themselves—any type of bottleneck is what you're looking for.

The problem with routine routes is that deer as often as not

Photo by Kenn Shrader

Photo by Richard P. Smith

Bowhunters and some gun hunters in private areas hunt undisturbed deer. Stands are best placed on routine travel routes.

Most gun hunters encounter deer that are moved by other hunters. The best bet may be a stand on a route deer use to evade people.

abandon them when they feel hunting pressure. Then whitetails take seemingly random evasion routes.

Evasion routes, of primary interest to most gun hunters, are not easily detectable. These routes are selected because of cover, terrain, and safety. Refer to the scouting chapter for more discussion on analyzing escape routes.

The best locations for routine-route stands are usually not too far back in the woods. Deer spend the most'time in "edge" areas — the transitions between vegetation types — and the farther you go in, the more deer you will alert. The best evasion-route stands are usually fairly far back where other hunters are reluctant to go, but again, take care not to disturb deer getting to the stand.

A Network of Stands

You'll probably want several good stands picked out, for several reasons: You may spook your buck at your primary stand and he will probably avoid the area after that. Someone else may move into your primary hunting area. You may simply want to have a change of scenery after hunting a particular stand for several days.

Select various stand sites to give yourself a variety of options for the times of day, times of season, and types of hunting you are doing. But don't set up stands carelessly just to have a bunch of stands. Pick each location as if it were your only one.

For many hunters, site selection is a simple matter of taking a stand that has traditionally produced deer. But most hunters don't have this luxury; they must analyze deer movements and compare the various tradeoffs of different stand locations.

For example, you may find a stand location that is among very heavy deer sign, but which

A network of stands in diverse locations can help you pick the best site for each deer hunting situation. Some good stand sites include (1) a hardwood ridge (2) a natural crossing where cover is closest on each side of an opening (3) a field edge (4) a brushy bedding area and (5) a thick creek bottom in an otherwise open area.

allows you to see only 20 yards in each direction. Another stand with good visibility may cover only marginal deer habitat, or it might be uncomfortable or too close to livestock. A deer hunter needs to have lots of options, weigh all the factors, and decide which would be the best place on opening morning.

Using your knowledge of when and where deer concentrate, and the "ideal stand" characteristics we have discussed, start selecting stand sites well before season. Prepare them so you can hunt there on short notice. Keep monitoring deer patterns in the area you are hunting, and select your primary stand accordingly.

Elements of a Good Deer Stand

Even with the advantages a stand gives the deer hunter, he must put all the cards in his favor. He must find a stand that is as favorable as possible, then make the site even more desirable.

Assuming you have chosen a location of good deer travel, make sure your stand has these other ingredients:

You must be able to see the deer and get a shot. No matter how well your site is selected, it is useless if you can't see and shoot a passing deer. Most good stands are in cover. But if you are in very thick woods, there may be only a few places where you could shoot at deer; that buck might pass without offering a shot. When you take stand on a deer evasion route, odds are the deer will be moving, and your chances for a shot will be further restricted.

As a rule, select a whitetail deer stand with cover that allows you to see as far as you can accurately shoot, and no more. This puts you in cover sufficient to attract deer, but without hampering your shooting opportunities. There are exceptions, such as if you are hunting from an elevated stand over a swamp or low brush, where you can see much farther than you can shoot.

Hunters who want to hunt heavy cover but extend their shooting range can clear shooting lanes. With a machete, axe, or saw, cut lanes through the brush extending for about 75 yards from your stand. These lanes are like the spokes of a wheel with your stand at the hub. Clear out some of the other brush around your stand, too, so you can see deer approaching the lanes. Don't get carried away and make the area look like a tornado just passed through, however, and be sure to have permission before doing any landscaping.

The shooting-lanes system can give you excellent shooting opportunities while hunting optimum cover. It is especially useful

Photos by Mike Strandlund

Set up stands with careful attention to deer travel patterns and your ability to get a shot. You may need to clear shooting lanes; if you hunt from a tree stand, you'll probably have to remove some high limbs.

to bowhunters, whose arrows are vulnerable to deflection by small twigs or even leaves.

The stand must be downwind or crosswind of the deer. You'll probably never see a deer that approaches from downwind. Even if you're using a tree stand, you've got to be 20 feet or more off the ground to ensure a downwind deer won't scent you. The blind or tree stand must be positioned so the deer cannot get your scent from the direction they are most likely to approach.

This means that you cannot just set up stands at random near deer sign. You must have an idea which way the deer are traveling so that you can locate stands where they can't scent you. In building permanent stands, keep the prevailing wind and the

The best blind is often no blind at all—just a cluttered backdrop to break up your outline, combined with absolute stillness. Deer hunters often make the mistake of using a blind that is so tight they have a hard time seeing and shooting deer.

thermals in mind. (Prevailing wind is from the west or north in most places; thermal air currents travel up slopes in morning and down in evening most of the time.) In good locations, have stands set up on each side of the deer's likely route to ensure you can be downwind or crosswind.

The stand must help prevent deer from seeing or hearing you. A whitetail hunter on stand must be still, quiet, and somewhat camouflaged. A good stand helps this; a poor one hinders it.

Stillness is critical for the hunter on a deer stand, because the whitetail's eyesight is so attuned to movement. Discomfort and restlessness are the main causes of movement that can warn a deer you don't even know is there. Seat pads and light stools help to prevent that movement.

While deer don't normally panic at small sounds, quietness is also very important. Noise gets a deer's immediate attention and may help him spot you. In ground blinds, clear noisy leaves and twigs away from your feet. In tree stands, be sure that shifting your weight does not cause the stand to creak.

Your stand must be accessible. Serious deer hunters get on their stands before light and leave stands after dark. This may require some woodsmanship if your stand is in a remote location. You must be able to access your stand without alerting the deer that you plan to hunt. Some stand sites that are otherwise ideal must be ruled out because they cannot be reached without disturbing the deer you would be hunting.

You can make a stand more accessible by locating it near a trail, logging road, creek, or other landmark you can follow. You may also mark the trail to and from your stand with surveyor's ribbon or similar material that you can follow with a flashlight.

Remember that you'll hopefully face the chore of getting your deer out. If you are hunting by yourself and have several good stand options, the prospects of a deer drag may be a major consideration in the stand you choose.

Photos by Mike Strandlund

A dilemma for the deer hunter is finding a prime stand he can get to and from in the dark. Blazing an access route with orange ribbon is usually the best approach. Be sure to remove the markers when you quit using the stand.

Preparing the Stand

There are big differences in stand hunting depending on the type of stand you use. Many whitetail hunters simply post, hiding next to a tree or bush, while others build elaborate blinds on the ground. Permanent tree stands are ever-increasing in popularity, and the portable tree stand has put a whole new perspective in stand hunting for whitetails.

Posts and Blinds

The simplest stand is to sit or stand in the open at a good vantage point — known in some regions as posting. You can also build a blind on the ground from nearby materials — usually dead branches, leafy vegetation, and pine boughs. Either approach may be better for your purposes depending on the situation.

Gun hunters who can hold still on stand are often better-off posting rather than sitting in a blind. Leaning against a large tree, the hunter's outline is camouflaged and he has no obstructions to sight and movement as he might have in a blind. It takes only stillness to hide from a whitetail at gun-hunting yardages.

Photo by Mike Strandlund

The posting hunter can follow the movements of deer through a cluttered forest and pick his shot.

Photo by Mike Strandlund

A good, natural blind in a prime location helps a hunter get close to deer. All blinds should incorporate some sort of gun rest to enhance the hunter's shooting ability.

Blinds are better in some cases. A hunter dressed in complete blaze orange against a dark woods is perceptible to nearby deer; he might have a better chance in a blind. Deer often walk into range of fully camouflaged bowhunters, but when it comes time to shoot, they need something to hide their movement.

The best blinds are simple and natural. A couple of bushes or a windfall make a good blind as long as they do not obstruct the hunter's movement or vision.

One favorite man-made design is the three-sided blind. Locate three trees growing in a group about six feet from each other. Pile dead wood against them to form three walls about three feet high. In rainy weather, some hunters use rope and water-repellent material to make a roof.

There are infinite blind designs. A couple of branches laid across a fallen log may be all you need. Or, you might purchase a commercial blind made of stakes and camouflage cloth.

All blinds should enhance your shooting ability. Blinds for gun hunters should always have a solid gun rest; to sit in a blind and shoot offhand is to ignore one of the best benefits of blind hunting. Archers benefit from high-walled blinds with several narrow, vertical shooting slots.

Tree Stands

A stand raised high off the ground gives the hunter a decided advantage. Sometimes these elevated stands are on a high bank or ridge, but normally they are tree stands.

The biggest advantages of the tree stand are that it maximizes visibility and minimizes the scent you leave on the ground. Since whitetails usually travel into the wind, they are most likely to approach the stander from the direction where they could catch his scent. If the hunter can divert most of his scent, he is much more likely to see deer.

A good tree stand also keeps deer from spotting you. As deer walk through woods, they scan the ground ahead for danger, but they seldom search the treetops. Another benefit for the gun hunter is that his blaze orange will blend much better with the sky than with a dark woods background.

Some hunters believe that tree stands put you above the deer's line of sight, because deer don't look up. This is a fallacy. Deer are quick to spot movement or the outline of a hunter skylined in a tree. In some areas where tree stands have been prevalent for many years, deer have become conditioned to watching for hunters in trees.

Tree stands fall into four categories: simple tree "posts," where the hunter just sits on a limb; permanent tree stands constructed of lumber; portable tree stands; and tower stands constructed where there are no trees.

A so-called tree post can be very efficient with the right tree. It offers an elevated stand with a minimum of effort and disturbance to the area. But a comfortable tree post is difficult to find. If you are uncomfortable you move more, and a moving hunter in a tree is very visible.

Permanent tree stands bridge the comfort gap. With a platform, seat, and railing, a good permanent stand can make the difference between a miserable and pleasant perch. Drawbacks of permanent stands are that they may require a lot of work and expense, and they are illegal in many places. Once you build your stand, you're stuck with that location. Poorly built permanent stands kill trees and create eyesores.

Portable tree stands furnish both comfort and freedom. Commercially manufactured of steel, portable stands come in many designs. They fall into two categories—self-climbing, and lock on, the latter of which requires a separate method of getting into the tree.

A permanent tree stand is secure and comfortable, allowing the whitetail hunter to keep still for many hours of hunting. Check the hunting regulations in your area before you build or use a permanent tree stand.

A tree post is quick and easy to use, but is usually uncomfortable and best suited to short stays.

Combining comfort, mobility, and safety, the portable tree stand has become the favorite of many whitetail hunters.

Photos by Jim Zumbo

Tower stands are an option for the deer hunter who wants an elevated position where large trees are scarce. While they are conspicuous, deer get used to them if they are placed far in advance of hunting season.

Portable units allow you to hunt from any acceptable tree on the spur of the moment. They let you decide which way you want to face and how high you want to go. Disadvantages are that they are sometimes noisy—both in carry and in use. Some designs are rather unstable and dangerous. Some climbing models are hard to use unless you are in superb shape. A few damage trees.

Of very limited use, mainly in the brush or swamp country of the South, are tower stands. Made of lumber or welded steel, towers provide the hunter with a "tree stand" where there are no trees. These conspicuous stands usually have some sort of blind to hide the hunter, and deer are not usually suspicious of them. They take a lot of time and money to build, but provide a beautifully unobstructed shooting area.

Using Tree Stands

Tree stand hunters must use extreme care to maximize success and safety.

A common mistake is to choose a tree stand site because of the tree rather than the deer sign. A lazy hunter may take a tree that is not in the best stand location simply because it has low, heavy limbs convenient for climbing, when he could greatly increase his chances with a little more effort.

Another error is to get too low or too high in the tree. A tree stand six or eight feet off the ground is much worse than a ground blind; you will be scented just as readily, and be much more visible. A stand too high puts you farther from the target and behind more branches. It is also unsafe and results in poor shooting angles. The optimum tree stand height is usually between 12 and 20 feet, depending on your type of hunting and the conditions.

Getting into the tree is often the tree stand hunter's major consideration. If you don't have stout limbs you can reach, you have to devise your own method. You can nail steps to the tree trunk, rope or wire climbing blocks to the trunk, or use screw-in tree

Photo by Gerald Almy

Secure steps, a safety belt, and a careful approach are mandatory for safety in the precarious business of using portables.

stand steps. Some hunter use ladders made of sawed and nailed saplings; others use a rope and perhaps some sort of grappling hook. There are other methods; the main thing is to avoid damaging the valuable trees and to ensure safety.

A harness securing you to the tree is a critical piece of tree stand safety equipment. It should go on before you start climbing and not come off until you return to the ground. If it must be removed momentarily as you climb over limbs, make sure you always keep a firm grip on the harness. Don't have more than a couple feet of free play in the harness, or you could be injured.

Tree stand hunters must also have a haul line to bring up gun and gear after securing themselves to the stand.

Stand-Hunting Methods

There's more to stand-hunting than sitting there till a deer comes by. Do your best to see the deer before it sees you. If the woods are very dry and still, you'll probably hear deer long before they are in sight. In this case, you can shift your weight and move a little on the stand. But if the day is damp or breezy, you must use extreme care; deer may approach silently. Scan the woods by shifting your eyes, not your head. When you must move, do so very slowly. You've got plenty of time.

Photo by Mike Strandlund

While on stand, keep still but watchful. Scan the area by moving your eyes, not your head. When you spot the deer you want, move very slowly into shooting position.

121

Stillness and keeping your scent away from your planned shooting area are the keys to getting close to whitetails while on stand.

You can avoid having to turn to watch your flanks by positioning your stand where you could hear deer approaching from behind. Whitetails always make noise walking through water, so a slow, shallow creek on your backside will monitor for you. A heavy carpet of dry leaves may accomplish the same thing.

Stay unseen. If your stand is on the ground, sit on the shady side of the tree. In the trees, stay close to the trunk and pay special attention to keeping still.

When you see deer, suppress the urge to lurch into shooting

position. Move deliberately, analyzing the best shooting opportunity by considering the deer's angle of travel, distance, and cover. If you see a deer you want to shoot, briefly scan the direction from where it came to make sure you are not being watched by another deer that could betray your presence.

It often takes many hours or many days before this opportunity arises. While stand hunting does not involve great stamina or skill, it is very challenging because of the perseverance it requires. Trail watching is the truest test of a whitetail hunter's patience, which is his most important attribute.

CHAPTER 7

STILL-HUNTING AND STALKING WHITETAILS

The still-hunter eases through prime whitetail bedding or loafing cover slowly and quietly, stopping, looking, and listening. He tries to be invisible to all the whitetail's senses, stealing up on a deer unaware or getting close enough for a shot before the deer is alerted.

The term still-hunting is confusing to many hunters; it sounds like the hunter should be unmoving, as on stand. Actually the word, developed over a century ago, signifies quietness of the hunter and stillness of the deer. It is indeed a "still" form of hunt-

Photo by Richard P. Smith

Only with the utmost care and concentration can a whitetail hunter consistently sneak within gun range before he is spotted by deer.

ing compared with the common practice then of running deer with hounds.

Still-hunting is a method that few hunters have mastered, for a simple reason: It puts the hunter at a distinct disadvantage. Deer can utilize their superior senses to full capacity, remaining still and undetected while the hunter sends out visual and auditory warnings as he moves through the woods. It is very difficult to spot a whitetail before it sees, hears, or scents you. The deer can then hide and let you pass, or bound away before you can shoot.

Yet, a still-hunt is intriguing. It holds a fascination for most of us, seeming like the "real" way to hunt deer. It is much more pleasant and stimulating than sitting for hours on a cold, uncomfortable stand. Still-hunting is an interesting, challenging way to hunt the whitetail, a very satisfying way to collect a trophy.

An Approach to Still-Hunting

Not all hunters make still-hunters, and not all situations are made for still-hunting. You need the right skills, attitude, and conditions.

There are two basic approaches to still-hunting. You can walk with a specific objective in mind, following a plan and systematically hunting familiar country. Or you can just ease along through any good-looking deer woods, hunting on speculation. Both approaches have merit, as long as you follow some essential still-hunting rules.

Preparation

Before you embark on a still-hunt, you have to be prepared. Since quietness is imperative, you should dress in the quietest clothes possible. Wool or flannel are best, muffling the sound of twigs and brush scuffing against your body. Nylon and similar synthetic fabrics are worst, popping and scraping each time they contact undergrowth. Even if it's raining, avoid wearing rainsuits on a still-hunt. Wool is much better; you'll get wet, but you'll stay warm.

Use footwear that is as light and soft as possible, allowing you to feel underfoot branches before they snap, and muffling smaller sounds. Sneakers, as the name implies, are among the best if the weather is not too cold. Some hunters actually hunt in wool socks with no shoes for the ultimate in quiet and sensitivity.

The still-hunter must be very careful to remain unseen by the prying eyes of deer, and should choose his clothing accordingly.

Photo by Wade Bourne

There are two basic approaches to still-hunting—simply easing through a good deer woods, or stalking good locations with a strategy in mind.

Complete camouflage clothing is a necessity for the bowhunter. Gun-hunters in snowy conditions are well-camouflaged; through a deer's eyes, their blaze orange blends well with the white snow. But the gun-hunter in a brown forest has a decision to make. The more blaze orange he wears, the more likely he'll be spotted. Once he's donned the legal requirement of blaze orange, the gun-hunter must decide if he wants to increase his safety margin or his chances for sneaking up on a deer, and dress accordingly.

Select your bring-along gear carefully before you head out. Next to his gun and cartridges, binoculars are the still-hunter's most important key to success. Depending on where you go and how long you'll be there, you may want a pack containing food, drink, map, compass, and other items.

Strategies for the Still-Hunter

Still-hunting involves a lot of time-consuming travel through places that have no deer, and through places where deer are virtually impossible to surprise. There are ways to improve your productive hunting time and to maximize chances of success when you step into an ideal still-hunting situation.

Certain strategies and tactics you can employ in still-hunting become apparent when you boil down your mission to the two essentials: staying undetectable to the deer's senses, and hunting in a place where there are shootable deer.

Wind Direction

The primary rule of still-hunting is to hunt into the wind. Unless the breeze is blowing into your face as you walk (either directly or at an angle) you are wasting your time. Your wafting scent will send danger signals throughout the woods in front of you. You can occasionally get closer to a deer that has seen or heard you, but your smell will always scatter whitetails.

Wind can be difficult to decipher. It's easy to keep track of stiff, steady air currents, but slight breezes can be fickle and deceiving. A shift in even a slight breeze will betray your presence.

As you still-hunt, constantly check the wind. Some hunters are skilled at monitoring wind direction just by the way it feels.

Photo by Mike Strandlund

A string tied to your bow or gun barrel lets you keep track of the wind direction while still-hunting.

Photo by Gerald Almy

A good still-hunting strategy is to sneak silently through thick cover until you come to a partial opening, then scan thoroughly for movements or parts of deer.

Others toss a bit of dust or grass into the wind, or watch a thread they keep tied to their guns or bows. The flame of a butane lighter or puff of powder also works well.

Walk, Stop, Look, and Listen

It takes a high degree of skill to be a successful still-hunter. The prime ingredients are patience, stealth, and a keen eye for game. Accomplished still-hunters typically take years to develop their technique.

If there's one secret to still-hunting, it is to move slowly. There is no such thing as moving too slowly when still-hunting the whitetail. How slow is slow? Taking 20 minutes to travel 100 yards is acceptable. Half that pace — three or four steps a minute — is better.

While you're learning to still-hunt, the pace seems agonizingly slow, but is necessary if you hope to ever walk up on a deer. A common misconception among deer hunters is that they must cover a lot of ground to increase their chances of coming up on a whitetail. But to cover a lot of ground, you have to do so quickly, and that puts the odds in the deer's favor. Good still-hunters measure distance in yards, not miles. You're much better off loitering through a few hundred yards of prime bedding habitat than hunting the woods and fields double-time all day long.

As you walk, stop frequently to listen and scan the area around you. The sounds and sights you search for are seldom the obvious noise of a walking deer or its full body. A flick of an ear or tail, the thud of a single footfall, a glint of sunlight from an antler — these are what the hunter seeks. It's a great advantage to use binoculars and scan as far ahead as possible. Search for a bit of shiny black or bright white, indicating a deer's eye, nose, or a bit of its underside. A white V may be a deer's tail, while a solid oval amidst a debris-covered hillside could be the outline

Photos by Leonard Lee Rue III

In most still-hunting situations, you'll be hunting hard-to-see bedded bucks that are watching for you. Only the most observant hunters with trained eyes can get a shot at deer like these.

of a bedded deer. Remember, to see these pieces of deer, you have to concentrate on *looking for pieces* of deer.

Novice hunters make the common mistake of looking for the entire body of a deer. This makes you miss the details and can cause you to overlook a deer just a few yards off. If the whole deer were visible, chances are it would have already spotted you and vacated the premises.

Always stop for a long pause when you reach an area where a whitetail could be camouflaged — such as thickets, blowdowns, and cutovers. Give the area a quick scan to look for the movement of a walking or running deer, then go back over and check it thoroughly. Sink to your knees and study the area again from a different perspective. Never proceed until you've investigated every nook and cranny for that telltale piece of deer.

On your hunt, you'll hear a myriad of crunching leaves and snapping twigs. At each suspicious sound, freeze everything but your eyeballs as they scrutinize every inch of cover at the origin of the sound.

If you believe you are still-hunting correctly but are still spooking deer before you see them, reconsider your approach. Are you keeping still enough during your pauses? The still-hunter must perfect the art of freezing in his tracks. Don't worry if you seem to get more than your share of bobbing white flags. Whitetails are so well camouflaged that most will be invisible. They cannot be seen no matter how hard you try. Try to keep quieter, walk

Photo by Mike Strandlund

This is the result most hunters get when they try to still-hunt the whitetail. To get closer you have to move slower and look harder.

slower, and look harder, and sooner or later you'll catch a deer making a mistake. You'll need to be alert to spot that one.

Still-Hunting Logistics

The way you move through the woods and the route you take involve those details that can make the difference in getting your deer. The wise still-hunter can identify and take advantage of every subtle opportunity to increase his chances.

Look for a quiet route to take as you head into the wind. If there's soft snow cover or the ground is wet, you need only to plot a route where you can avoid brushing against thick undergrowth. You should be able to walk through fairly thick cover, however, moving so slowly that you can quietly take each twig and hold it aside as you pass. Don't be above dropping to your hands and knees to crawl when it will help your cause.

Many deer-hunting days begin with the forest floor covered by crackly frost. Take a stand until the frost melts, leaving the ground soggy and perfect for still-hunting.

With dry, snowless ground, you may be able to find a path free of dry leaves and twigs. This could be a cow path, grassy

NRA Staff Photo

Walking quiet, untraveled trails, poking occasionally into the thick stuff, is a good way to still-hunt unexplored territory.

area, or an old logging road. Some hunters don hip boots and wade quietly among slow-moving creeks. Fast water can cover your sound but also make it impossible to hear a deer approach. Also, whitetails tend to avoid areas where their senses are hampered.

Pine stands offer some of the best concealment for the still-hunter. Vegetation stays thick even in late fall. A soft carpet of fallen needles muffles your footsteps.

If conditions are perfect, you may enjoy the very quietest form of still-hunting—over bare ice. In northern states, deer season often coincides with the first hard freezes. Thick ice forms on swamps, beaver ponds, and slow creeks, enabling you to access otherwise impenetrable deer cover in complete silence. In a swampy, ice-covered beaver colony, you can slide gingerly in and out of the channels and guts to search for deer bedded in the swamp grass. You might work the fringes of a frozen lake, or slip along an irrigation ditch between feeding fields. Just be aware of the obvious dangers of walking on ice and use extreme care.

Coping with Noisy Woods

A forest floor cluttered with crunchy leaves and brittle sticks does not necessarily rule out still-hunting. At a rate of four or five steps a minute, you have plenty of time to consider where and how to place your foot. You can avoid fallen branches and set down each foot with slow, even pressure that minimizes the crackling of leaves. Some hunters pull heavy wool socks over their shoes. The fabric pads the step and muffles the crunch.

An alternative to walking quietly is to sound like something else. When something is sneaking up on a deer and accidentally makes a noise, the deer can tell that sound was made by a stalking predator. Sounds with an air of nonchalance are less frightening.

If you're hunting in turkey country, you might try this: Carry a diaphragm or pushbutton turkey call and let out a soft cluck every few steps. Humans and turkeys sound the same when they walk, and a deer that hears your footsteps may dismiss the sound when it hears a turkey call. Whitetails know that turkeys are very

Photo by Mike Strandlund

You can deceive a deer into thinking your footsteps are those of a turkey if you sound a turkey call every few steps. Don't use this tactic in turkey season!

wary, and the call may actually give the deer more confidence. Of course, avoid this tactic during combined deer/turkey seasons.

Another approach when it's impossible to be quiet is to sound like a squirrel. Bushytails make a distinctive *tish-tish, tish-tish* sound as they pounce through the leaves. You can make the same sound by softly shuffling your boot as you place it down. The sound shouldn't be much louder than a normal footstep.

Keeping Out of Sight

A whitetail may walk within arm's length without spotting you, as long as you're still, but it can see you take a step from a quarter-mile away. This poses the major threat to a good still-hunter, who cannot avoid the fact that he must move.

Stay off fields and narrow ridgetops, and don't hunt down a ridge toward a facing slope. You are sure to be spotted. In general, it's best to hunt edges, staying just inside the thicker cover and looking for deer in the more open areas. This way you are hidden, the deer are visible, and you have the best shooting opportunity.

Sneaking along, use the cover and terrain to your best advantage. Watch for depressions in the topography that you can approach while hidden, staying hidden until you're as close as possible. This holds true for sneaking over ridgetops and river banks. Fencelines, thickets, old road grades, and many other types of cover and terrain allow invisible approaches.

Your frequent pauses while still-hunting should always place you next to a large tree. Stand in its shadow as you listen and scan for signs of deer. The tree may hide you or at least break up your outline. It will also provide a gun rest if a shooting opportunity should arise.

Bucks in thick cover can rather easily hide or sneak from a lone still-hunter. For this reason, you must thoroughly sweep good bedding areas or chance walking past your deer. The best method for this is to zig-zag into the wind, walking crosswind on each of your quartering passes.

There are several other considerations for your approach. Carry your gun in a ready position—never on a sling. On bright days, try to keep the sun at your back—but never at the cost of unfavorable wind direction. If the sun is in your face and hampering your vision, make your pauses in the shade of large trees.

Still-Hunting Familiar Territory

Your odds of pulling off a still-hunt take a giant leap when you hunt areas you've scouted with the purpose of planning a still-hunt. Make note of the bedding areas you want to investigate, the scrapes you want to check, the hollows you want to stalk. Then, keeping the prevailing winds in mind, mentally rehearse your approach to hunting the area. Plan to make use of the available trails to hide your sound and the cover to hide you from sight.

Learn or deduce what the deer will do, and plan your approach around that. For example, if deer are moving off a field, through a woods, and into a bedding area in the morning, plan your hunt to intercept them at certain places at the times they should be there.

Still-Hunting Unfamiliar Territory

As noble as it is to scout and plan, most hunters find themselves still-hunting in unfamiliar country. This puts you at a disadvantage, but is a good way to learn the territory and its deer.

There are a few tactics that can help you here. One is to find a good whitetail feeding area such as a field or oak grove, then get on a good trail that appears to head for bedding cover. Follow it carefully. Somewhere toward the end of that trail is what you're looking for.

As you gain experience still-hunting, you'll learn to recognize places you encounter that are most likely to hold deer. You'll learn how to approach them.

Some hunters are reluctant to still-hunt strange terrain because of fear they'll get lost. If you're unwilling to strike off into the woods, there are ways to hunt with confidence in your location. An easy way is to walk a fenceline, powerline, or old road. You can also stay within sight of a landmark like a lake, stream, or distinct mountaintop. Carry a topo map and a compass, and check them from the moment you set foot in the woods.

Still-Hunting Specific Terrain

While the fundamentals of still-hunting always remain the same, there are special tactics you can use for hunting certain types of terrain.

Bedding Areas

Thick bedding areas, especially small thickets overlooked by other hunters, are among the best places for still-hunts. The problem is that the heavy cover makes shooting difficult.

If you've scouted the area, you may have discovered an ap-

Photo by Leonard Lee Rue III

Photo by Mike Strandlund

Thick bedding areas are among the best places for a still-hunt. Snow cover helps you move quietly and spot the dark shapes of deer.

proach or two that will allow a shot at a flushing deer. There might be an open area or two in the center. Or you could work just inside the thick part, hoping for a deer to run out into the open surrounding the thicket. Where legal, buckshot is often the best load in these situations.

Since good bedding sites are so good for still-hunting and are usually small, you can be extra careful and take more time hunting them. You might even catch a buck napping.

Ridgelines
You might find yourself hunting a long ridgeline. With the food, cover, and relative inaccessibility they provide, these are often prime places for the still-hunter. As the day warms, air rises and these thermal air currents keep your scent away from deer below you.

Rather than walking the ridge, sneak along just under the crest on one side for a while, then creep over the top hoping to find deer that could not see, hear, or smell you because of the cover the ridgeline provided. Mountain whitetails often bed just below a ridgeline.

Still-Hunting Edges
Whitetails are edge animals, preferring the transitional zones where many habitat types come together. A wise still-hunter uses this to his advantage. Where wind is favorable, you can hunt through an area where the walking is better, looking for deer in the thicker adjacent cover. For instance, there might be a plantation of big pines surrounded by a thornbush thicket. The easy walking in the pines allows you to silently probe the edges of the thicket at various points.

Photo by Mike Strandlund

Encountering Deer
Catching a big buck unaware in his bed is the supreme achievement of the still-hunter. Good still-hunters can regularly discover deer before deer discover them, but in most cases, the deer will see you first.

Most still-hunters encounter deer just as they bolt for safety. It's important to be quick but cautious with a gun, and to pick your shots carefully.

Most successful still-hunts involve the hunter getting very close before the deer sees him and bolts. The hunter is taken by surprise, but has enough composure and skill to bring down the game.

The key here is being prepared and able to make instant decisions. You have to identify bucks quickly and pick your shots well. Mentally rehearse situations, and always consider safety and the chances of poorly wounding game when making your shoot/don't-shoot decisions.

Stalking Whitetails

Generally considered our most intelligent hoofed game animal, the whitetail uses every bit of cover possible for concealment from hunters. Unlike many other big game, whitetails are very seldom caught out in the open where they can be deliberately stalked. There are exceptions, however. Stalking is fairly common in open areas of the West. Undisturbed eastern whitetails may be spotted and stalked where they come onto fields at dusk, or in big, open woods.

More often the whitetail may be spotted out of gun range by

Photo by Wade Bourne

Whitetails can occasionally be spotted in the open and stalked. A hunter may stalk to the animal itself, or to a point where he can intercept the traveling deer.

Photo by Mike Strandlund

Sneaking up on ever-wary whitetails is an art few hunters have mastered. The sight and sound cover offered by a cornfield is a great advantage.

a still-hunter. The animal may be in sight, or it may have walked out of sight, and the hunter must try to sneak close enough for a shot.

Wind direction is obviously the main consideration before starting a stalk. Get downwind and move as quickly as you can at first while making sure you can't be spotted. Bucks don't expose themselves for very long at a time, and may move off if you dawdle.

As you approach, you'll feel yourself enter that critical zone where the tiniest mistake will panic the deer—that zone where the whitetail's senses pick up the smallest signal. Here the stalk becomes painstaking as you ease ahead with extreme stealth and care.

Watch the deer's body language. Feeding whitetails have a way of twitching their tails that signifies all is well. They will periodically snap their heads up, trying to catch the movement of a predator that may be stalking them. Time your movements to coincide with the deer looking down or away. Always be prepared to freeze when the head snaps up.

Take care to use all available cover and to keep as close to the ground as possible. Scan the area for other deer that may spot you. Hide anything shiny or otherwise visible, or leave it behind. If you have no headnet or camo makeup on your face, use a bandanna or other covering. Pull your cap down tight, or cover your face with a glove when the deer looks your way.

Chances are the deer will be alerted by sound rather than sight. It probably won't bolt, but rather stare in your direction for a few moments. It may feign lowering its head and then jerk it back up, hoping to catch you off guard. If the sound you made was slight, the deer will probably forget about it in a few minutes. If you snapped a large twig or made a similar heavy noise, the deer may know there is danger lurking and leave. You must decide if you are in range for a shot.

Sometimes during a stalk you can plot the course of a deer as it slowly moves along. In that case it may be better to stalk toward a point in the deer's path and wait.

Tracking and "Hounding"

Among the most difficult methods of whitetail hunting is to get on a deer's track and follow with enough stealth or persistence to make the kill. Tracking is a term for following a fresh set of hoofprints, being quiet and alert, hoping to sneak up on the deer. Another method is hounding, known among the old-timers as running down a deer. This is trailing a deer that knows it is being followed, and staying with it until it makes a mistake.

Tracking is difficult because whitetails watch their backtrails for hunters and predators doing just that. Running down a whitetail is only for the most tenacious and woods-wise hunters, and is practiced very seldom today.

Snow is a requirement for trailing a whitetail for any distance. It's best to locate a fresh track at first light after a snowfall the night before—preferably one that ended just a couple hours earlier. Try to determine how old the trail is, then make up for lost time at first, slowing when you think you might be getting within a few hundred yards of the deer.

Watch as far ahead as possible. Since the ground is snow-covered, it should be fairly easy to spot deer. When entering a patch of thick cover, circle around and approach the thicket from a flank; you may avoid the prying eyes of a buck watching his backtrail.

Do your best to get a shot the first time you jump the deer.

Photo by Leonard Lee Rue III

Photo by Mike Strandlund

Tracking is an advanced form of whitetail hunting, requiring good knowledge of deer behavior and woodsmanship for success. Bucks are hard to trace to their beds, keeping a sharp eye on their backtrails.

If you don't, you'll be in for a long, difficult chase—the realm of running 'em down.

Very few hunters today attempt to chase down whitetails, though it seems this was a fairly common practice in the north during decades past. The idea was to start early and flush the deer time and again through the day. From curiosity, weariness, or diminished alarm, deer would sometimes let their persistent pursuer get closer until he got close enough.

This form of hunting requires the utmost in stamina and woodsmanship skills, along with perfect snow cover and a very big woods with few hunters. Which is why it is a lost art.

CHAPTER 8
DEER DRIVING

Photo by Richard P. Smith

Driving is the most efficient way for a group of dedicated deer hunters to load a meat pole. Planning is the key to drives that produce results like this.

Deer driving consists of one or more hunters moving through cover trying to chase the game toward standers. A good drive is, plain and simple, the most effective means to take whitetails. Even so, many hunters choose not to hunt this way. Some hunters prefer less-complex, more solitary and challenging ways to hunt the whitetail, even at the expense of filling their tag. Driving is more restrictive, complicated, and dangerous than other types of deer hunting. But it is an action-packed approach to deer hunting dependent on skill and teamwork. Driving can be an exciting, no-nonsense way of taking whitetails.

Deer and Driving

First and foremost, deer are not "driven." Perhaps if you could encircle a whitetail in fairly open ground with hunters every 20 feet, you could push a buck exactly where you wanted him to go. But most people don't hunt in groups the size of the National Guard. Most deer drives are made with under a dozen hunters—more commonly two to six.

Whitetails have highly refined survival instincts, one of which is the ability to deal with deer drives. And they learn fast. A buck that was duped by a drive and got away will not likely be fooled again.

Deer react to drives several ways. Many hunters have the mistaken belief that when whitetails sense drivers approaching, they flee the opposite direction right into the laps of standers. But more bucks will sneak or lie still than run. When they do run, they tend to take the most direct route to safety. Deer prefer to do so under cover, but will *not* hesitate to run in the open, as many hunters think. Don't mistakenly believe a river will serve as a natural barrier to deer—whitetails readily swim if they think they are being chased.

Whitetails are so able to elude groups of human hunters that their escape movements can seldom be controlled. Thus, trying to move deer to a certain place is for the most part futile. Emphasis should instead be placed on driving a manageable piece of real estate and strategically positioning standers *where the deer want to go.*

Matching Party and Place

The size of the hunting party should be considered in all aspects of a deer-drive hunt. The piece of land driven must not be too

Photo Courtesy Texas Parks and Wildlife Dept.

Photo by Leonard Lee Rue III

Whitetails react to drives by hiding or running. Set up the drive so hunters are prepared to take both types of deer.

Photo by Richard P. Smith

Drivers and standers must have a clear understanding of their roles in a deer drive. The best marksmen are the best standers and the most physically fit are the best drivers, though members of the hunting party usually take turns driving and standing.

large, or deer will easily elude hunters. It should not be too small, or you're wasting time and manpower. Most important is that the hunters do not try to cover too much area. Standers may be up to 200 yards apart or only 50, depending on the denseness of the cover; drivers may be 15 to 100 yards apart. If drivers or standers are too spread, deer will invariably slip through. A good example took place a few years ago in a northern state. About a dozen hunters spent several days driving a huge swampy woods in good deer country. They saw not a single buck. The group expressed its concerns to the DNR, which later conducted a deer population survey using a "control" drive with a huge number of people. Their findings: The area contained many bucks, many of them old and smart. The group of hunters had simply tried to cover too much area, and those old bucks gave them the slip.

Don't make your drives too long, either. Some hunters have the mistaken belief that if they make a two-mile push, they will pick up deer all along the way and end up with a "cattle drive" situation by the time they reach standers. Whitetails are too smart for this. You may be able to push deer straight ahead for a short distance, but it won't be long before they find a way out. Very long drives are a waste of effort and valuable hunting time.

General rules for setting up deer drives: Drivers should be spaced just within sight of each other. Standers should be far enough apart that they can easily see and shoot in their own area, with no overlap. Standers may be close enough that they can see each other, making sure that no deer gets through unseen. Or they may be spread out, covering most of the land and all the typical escape routes. All drives should have flankers watching for deer trying to escape the drive laterally.

A Deer-Drive System

A driving party must have a leader if it is to be organized and efficient. The leader must have a day-long or even season-long plan to make the most efficient use of time and manpower. He must know the areas to be driven or take the advice of fellow hunters who do. He should know the strengths and weaknesses of each party member, sending the most physically fit on the toughest walks and positioning the best marksmen where shots are the most difficult. Finally, he must be considerate and listen to the concerns of his party; their enjoyment is the ultimate goal of the hunt.

Well before hunting season, members of the party should be locating and getting access to prime areas for deer drives. Hunt clubs that stay in a certain area should get together and scout their area for the best ways of conducting drives at various sites. Then, prior to the hunt, list these locations and develop a plan to cover them as efficiently as possible. Map the areas and hunt them in a sequence that makes best use of time and travel.

Photo by Mike Strandlund

Organization is important for safety and success on a deer drive. Maps, meeting times, and logistics must be arranged well for best use of hunting time.

Arrangements must be made for meeting times, methods of transportation, and access to stands and driving lanes. In big, remote areas, each hunter should have a map. Consider how your party can communicate, take deer out, and deal with emergencies and lost hunters.

How to Drive Deer

Many hunting parties start the day with each man posting on a favorite stand, meeting a couple hours after daybreak to start driving. Posting takes advantage of the deer's natural morning movements, and can be more productive than driving this time of day. Large hunting parties may have to forego this step for sake of smoothness of operation.

At the hunt site, the leader outlines the plan. Drives should always be made with the wind or crosswind. They should go from wider to narrower cover, but not at the expense of driving into the wind, in which deer are very difficult to push past standers. The leader points out each hunter's duties; standers and drivers go their separate ways and take their positions.

There are several crucial elements at set-up. Standers must be quiet getting to their positions and avoid disturbing the area that is to be driven. The stand line must set up downwind or crosswind of the area to be driven; otherwise deer will scent standers and try to sneak out the sides or back through the drivers. It's fine if drivers get shots, but drivers are much easier than standers for deer to pinpoint and avoid.

It is also very important that drivers allow standers enough time to get in position. On long pushes of a mile or so, the drivers may start as soon as they get in position, which saves time. On more typical drives of under a quarter-mile, they should wait until they know standers are in place, or risk moving deer past an unoccupied stand. In downwind drives through small wedges of cover, drivers should not even begin to get in position until standers are set up; otherwise deer will scent the drivers and move out past empty stands. Before the drivers split up, they should calculate the maximum amount of time it would take the standers to get set up, then synchronize their watches and start moving at the predetermined time.

Photo by Irene Vandermolen, Rue Enterprises

Bucks may slip through undetected if avenues of escape go uncovered, or if standers are not given enough time to get into position.

Photo by Richard P. Smith

Standers on a deer drive should be posted at a good vantage point near a probable deer escape route. They should know where other standers are positioned for safety reasons.

Standers

On a typical drive, standers are positioned in a straight line or in the shape of a "C" cupped toward the driven area. There should also be flankers along the edges of the driven area watching for deer trying to escape laterally. The shooter's territory should extend as far as he can accurately shoot or get a bullet safely through cover.

Photo by Mike Strandlund

Since driven deer are usually on the run, hunters should be good shots on moving targets. Posters should set up near small openings and anticipate shooting situations.

Standers should have a general idea of how the stand line is laid out. This will prevent unsafe firing and keep a stander from taking a long, chancy shot at a deer that may be heading directly toward a fellow hunter.

Each individual stander is responsible for positioning himself with the best advantage possible. Ideally, he is covering an area that allows a good field of view and good shooting lanes (not at the expense of letting thickets go uncovered, however). Each stander should make note of deer trails, probable escape routes, terrain, and cover, anticipating where deer are likely to run and what types of shots he is likely to get. If there is a swath of very thick cover near his stand site, he should set up close to it. Deer are most likely to cross there, and will be difficult to hit unless he is close.

The stander should clear his stand site of major shooting obstructions, try to find a good rifle rest, and hide or keep very still. Tree stands can be an advantage, giving the hunter more visibility and making him less detectable, and adding an extra margin of safety because of the downward shooting angle. Bow-hunters usually use tree stands when driving deer. But except for those permanent stands set up in long-established drive areas, tree stands are not practical for most gun hunters on deer drives.

Many hunting parties organize deer drives that terminate at an old road, powerline, or other long, narrow opening between woods. The standers in this case should hide at the woods edge *toward* the drivers. This way, as deer break through the opening, hunters have a few moments to prepare for the shot, then can shoot safely away from the other standers. If standers are at the woods line across the opening, they will likely not get their sights on the deer until it is in line with other hunters and ready to re-enter cover. Then it's too late to shoot.

Standers should know how long the drive will take, and must be careful that shots they take at deer may not hit a driver.

Drivers

A driver's main job is to move deer to the standers. But in most cases, he is also a hunter. If they do their job properly, drivers will have nearly as good a chance at a shot as the standers will. This means driving as if they were still-hunting.

A good plan is to end a drive at an unused road, powerline, or other open corridor. Position standers on the edge facing the drivers so they have time to see and shoot at deer as they cross without the danger of pointing in the direction of another stander.

Old-time deer drives were typically noisy affairs, with shouts, whistles, even banging pots and pans every step of the way. This tradition still holds in some deer camps. But it is seldom the most effective technique. A noisy drive puts deer at a decided advantage. Deer know exactly where each driver is. They hear drivers coming a long way off. Deer are alerted rather than frightened by the noise. They have time to figure out what is going on, and can pinpoint drivers and sneak between them.

Conversely, a silent deer drive often catches deer off guard. They are more apt to panic and run directly into a stander or another silent driver. Deer have difficulty locating individual drivers, which makes it more difficult to sneak around or back through.

The silent treatment should begin even as hunters are setting up their drive line. Deer may be jumped at any time and hunters should always be prepared. As the drive commences, hunters ideally can see each other or, if the cover is so thick they can't see, they should be close enough to each other that they can hear an occasional footstep of the next driver. Communication in the form of an occasional whistle or shout may be necessary to keep the drive line intact, but drivers should otherwise walk quietly. Some hunting groups communicate with crow calls. Others use walkie-talkies, but these are illegal in some areas.

There are different theories concerning the optimum shape of the drive line. Most hunters try to keep a straight line with all hunters advancing at the same pace. Some form a V with the top ends of the V facing the standers; the theory here is that deer may be "trapped" more easily between drivers. Also, drivers in a regimented V formation can take shots to their left or right, depending on their position, with less possibility of endangering another driver. Theoretically, the hunter at the bottom of the V can shoot to either side or behind the drive. With a V-shaped drive line, however, you need more drivers to cover the same area, and it is more difficult for drivers to keep track of each other.

If you're driving through an area with a steady crosswind, it may be an advantage to form a slanted drive line. With wind coming from the right, the left side of the line should slant forward. This way, as hunters on the right flush deer, they may run downwind straight into a hunter they cannot smell. Flankers on the right watch for deer that flush the other direction. With this method, you don't need flankers on the left side of the drive, which lets you cover a larger area with the available hunters.

Photo by Mike Strandlund

Drivers must set up carefully and keep track of each other to ensure the drive is conducted as efficiently as possible.

With the drive moving downwind, the shape of the drive line makes little difference in the probability of drivers getting shots. The most important consideration is that drivers can see each other whenever possible, and that the line is kept straight so drivers know the location of all members of the party. **All hunters on drives must fully understand that no shots are to be taken if there is the remotest possibility of another hunter somewhere in the background.** On large drives, the drivers will have only small areas in which they can shoot with complete safety, such as directly behind. All drivers must adhere strictly to these safety rules.

Flankers

Flankers are those hunters watching for deer that try to squirt out the sides of the drive. Flankers may take posts on each side of the drive, or they may stroll along with the drivers, at the same pace but 50–100 yards ahead. Flankers usually cover a wide area and should be good shots.

Photo by Dave Murrian, Tennessee Wildlife Resources Agency

Whitetails can quickly figure out what a deer drive is about and try to slip out the side. Here is where the flanker comes into play.

Types of Drives

There are as many types of drives as there are types of terrain and types of hunting parties. Bigger drives, with over a half-dozen hunters, are designed to somewhat control the movement of the

155

deer and effectively trap deer between hunters. Small drives, with under a half-dozen hunters, are intended to get the deer up and moving toward a stander or two who know the area and where deer are likely to run.

Each different situation requires special techniques for optimum results. Following are some types of situations that deer drivers encounter; keep the general rules for driving in mind, and follow these tips for special situations.

Big Drives

Woodlot Drive. This is probably the most common type of drive. Depending on the cover, 10 hunters may be able to cover a woodlot of about 30 acres. With open surroundings, three standers and a flanker on each side should be able to handle the posting. It's more important to have enough drivers to adequately sweep the cover. Five drivers push through, heading downwind.

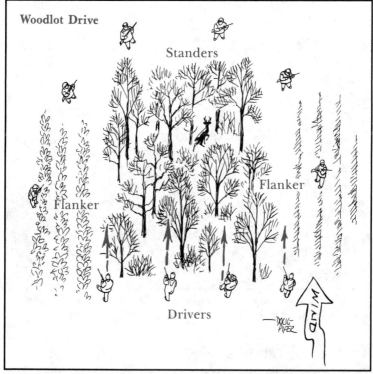

In the traditional woodlot drive, standers and flankers surround a woods while drivers move through quietly in a fairly straight line. Drivers should travel with the wind to keep deer from shying from standers.

Long Creekbottom in Fields. Just the opposite of the first situation, this requires more standers and less drivers. Two or three drivers should be able to cover a narrow creekbottom. The same number should be posted at the end of the drive. The remainder should be posting or moving flankers watching for deer making a break through the open fields. A buck may go in a straight line down the creekbottom the first time he is jumped, but the second time he is likely to decide to vacate his riverbed retreat.

Big Remote Forest. Even with a large party, hunters must restrict their area to a manageable size. Start by considering natural barriers or attractions. You can limit the deer's escape routes somewhat by conducting drives near highways, cliffs, and other geographical obstructions. By the same token, you can assume deer will head for a clearcut or other dense cover when pushed. These factors will help you decide where standers are needed and not needed. The stand line and the drive line should cup toward each other to minimize the game's ability to escape laterally. Be sure to have flankers walking about 75 yards ahead of each end of the drive line.

Cornfield Drive. Standing cornfields, often overlooked by deer hunters, harbor amazing numbers of deer after hunting season begins. But because they are usually large and very dense, they can be very difficult to drive. One approach is to drive part of the field with the entire group initially, using all your manpower to get the deer to one end of the field. Deer in such dense cover will not leave if they are not pushed too hard; they will just try to sidestep the drivers. Drive with the rows, each driver three or four rows apart and crossing over into the next row occasionally. Then take out just enough hunters to cover the end of the field from stands while the rest continue to drive. Hunters driving a cornfield should not shoot except at deer directly behind them.

Drive From Stand. If hunters know an area well, the drive from stand system works well. One group of hunters takes early-morning stands in one area, and another group in another area about a half-mile away. At a designated time, all hunters in one group get up and begin driving toward the other group. This system works well for two reasons: Deer are not likely to be disturbed and move out of the area just as the drive begins, and it makes good use of time. This is a good system for hunt clubs.

Dogs and Drives. In some areas of the South, dogs are a traditional part of deer drives. Dogs can be a definite aid in getting deer moving, and any big-running breed of dog will do. The prob-

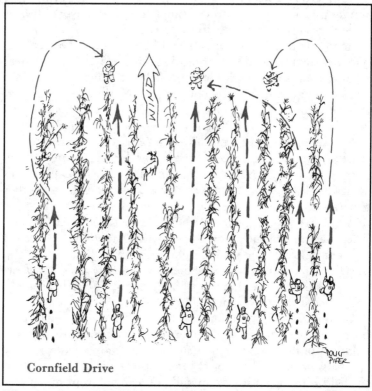

Cornfield Drive

When hunting pressure increases, deer find shelter in cornfields. Cornfields are hard to drive; you can make more use of your manpower by having some hunters start as drivers on each flank, then hurry around as the drive nears its end to become standers.

lem is that they can be hard to manage, slowing the group down. If they get hot on the trail of deer, hunters may face difficult shots at high-speed deer.

Small Drives

Bedding Area Drive. Two or more hunters can put on an effective drive through a bedding area if they know the place well. Standers circle downwind of the area while the drivers go to the upwind side. Standers hopefully know where major escape routes are and post there. Drivers walk quietly into the area, milling around, letting deer pick up their scent.

Still-Hunt Drive. This type of drive violates a main principle of deer drives: It has no standers. But it is quite effective for skilled

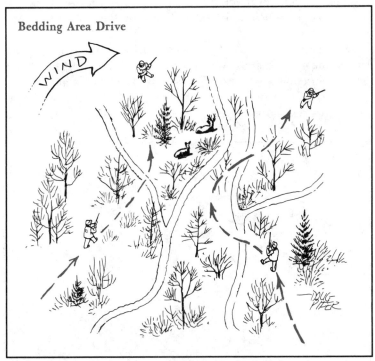

Bedding Area Drive

Thick bedding areas are often the best location for a small-group drive. A couple hunters can cover likely escape routes while a couple more meander through the area. The drivers may still-hunt and have a good chance at a shot.

hunters. The idea is to steal up on a deer and get a shot, or flush it to a fellow hunter who is being sneaky enough to get close. Hunters spread farther apart than normal deer drivers, in a zig-zagging line. They move slowly as if still-hunting; they should cover no more than a half-mile in an hour. Ideally, the terrain contains prime bedding areas, and all hunters know it well. A useful tactic is for a hunter or two to drop behind the other hunters. They may pick up deer that lie hidden until the other hunters pass, then get up and double back. With this type of drive, hunters must move upwind or crosswind.

Funnel Drive. Occasionally you will find a small patch of cover wide at one end and narrow at the other — perfect for a small deer drive. A small group may begin the drive at the wide end. Then as the cover narrows, and well before the end, a hunter or two may peel off and jog to the narrow end to become a stander. Remember that the narrow end must be downwind, and don't place too much faith in deer following the cover all the way to the point.

Draw Drive. This is a very effective drive for open, hilly country. It's the most common way of driving mule deer, but also works where whitetails are found. Find a brushy draw on a hillside and have a stander or two circle to the top; since most draws narrow at the top, few standers are needed. Two or three drivers enter

Funnel Drive

An ideal driving situation is where a patch of cover narrows toward the end of the drive. It may be covered by just a couple hunters, who may even help drive the wide part before circling to become standers.

the bottom of the draw and work their way to the top. If the draw bottoms out in a creekbottom or other brushy area, the drivers may first mill around through there, hoping deer will move into the draw and be trapped when the drive commences. This drive must be performed in the morning, when thermals are moving upward. You may drive down the draw in the evening, but this is usually not as productive. Whitetails prefer to escape uphill, and there is usually too much cover at the bottom of a draw for a small drive.

Stalk/Drive. If two hunters spot a deer, one circles around to the most likely escape route while the other stalks the deer. Either hunter may get a shot. To avoid being scented, hunters should both be crosswind of the deer.

Musical Chairs Drive. This is a unique way to hunt, combining stand-hunting, still-hunting, and driving. Hunters begin

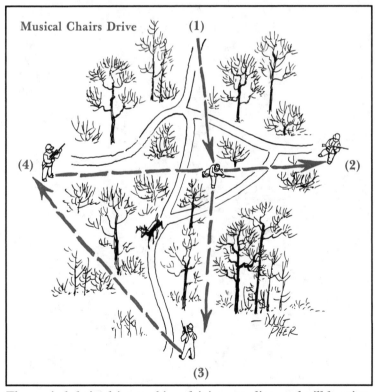

The musical chairs drive combines driving, standing, and still-hunting. Hunters take turns walking through a central bedding area and pushing deer toward companions.

the day taking stands on trails going into the same general deer bedding area. The stands surround the area, and each hunter knows exactly where the others are positioned. At a predetermined time (usually a couple hours after daybreak) one or two hunters get out of their stands and still-hunt toward other standers. When they get there, they take the post and the next stander or standers get up and walk toward the other hunters. With hunters crisscrossing the bedding area, deer are bound to be pushed toward standers.

CHAPTER 9

TACTICS FOR HUNTING THE WHITETAIL RUT

While a whitetail buck is always a difficult challenge, he is more vulnerable to hunting during his breeding season. A buck is much more active this time of year, often on the move all day long. The need to breed occupies much of his attention that is otherwise directed toward survival. His single-mindedness makes him susceptible to tricks used by hunters who understand the whitetail rut. These factors greatly improve a hunter's chance of getting close and getting a shot.

Just about any hunting season, from mid-September to January, coincides with a phase of the rut. When most hunters think of hunting the rut, they think of the peak of the rut — those few weeks in late fall when bucks and does are most active

Photo by Leonard Lee Rue III

Both bucks and does are easier to hunt when breeding season distracts them from their wariness and keeps them moving throughout the day.

and least wary. This peak of the rut is usually mid-November in most states, though it occurs in December or later in parts of the far South. There are also regional variations in the peak of the rut tied to differences in genetics and elevation.

In most areas, the rut's peak coincides with bowhunting season, and in a few places, the muzzleloader season. With few hunters roaming about, deer are seldom disturbed during these seasons. Their movements are natural. This is where hunters can employ special techniques to hunt rutting deer.

If the main rut coincides with regular firearms season in your area, the many hunters in the woods will quickly get the bucks' attention, regardless of the rut. Special techniques like rattling, calling, and fake scrapes may not work when there is heavy hunting pressure.

The rut progresses through several phases as hormone levels in deer build up, then drop off. These phases occur at different times in different parts of the country, according to latitude, elevation, and other factors. Throughout these stages the behavior of both bucks and does changes, and hunting tactics should change along with them.

Prebreeding Stage

As fall approaches and days shorten, the decrease in daylight triggers a surge of testosterone in whitetail bucks. The increase of this male hormone brings about physical and mental changes in the deer.

Among the first changes are the shedding of antler velvet and hardening of antlers, along with a buck's feeling the need to advertise stud service. Bucks begin rubbing their antlers on small trees, sometimes thrashing them violently. The rubbing scrapes off annoying shreds of velvet. It prepares the buck for fighting in the same way sparring helps a boxer — by strengthening the buck's neck muscles and helping him learn to use his antlers. Rubs also serve as signposts — by the visual rub marks and the scent the buck leaves from the glands near his eyes and forehead.

Hunters can use rubs to plan tactics and select stand sites. While bucks make rubs at random, a series of rubs may indicate a travel pattern of a certain buck. For instance, a rubbed sapling may show the direction a buck enters or leaves his bedding area or a field. The buck may never rub that tree again, but chances are he regularly passes through the area. Some whitetail bucks use trails quite frequently — especially young bucks early

Photo by Leonard Lee Rue III

At the onset of breeding season, whitetail bucks begin rubbing their antlers on small trees to mark territories and train for fighting. The size of the tree rubbed is often in proportion to the size of the buck.

Photo by Mike Strandlund

Rubs are not always good stand sites, but they can give valuable clues as to where, when, and how a buck is traveling.

Photo by Kenneth J. Forand, University of Georgia

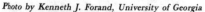

Whitetail bucks may start making scrapes a month or more before the rut peaks. Like rubs, these small scrapes simply mark a buck's turf and are seldom revisited.

in the season. If you find rubs appearing now and then along a certain trail, you may have found the closest thing to a sure-fire deer stand. It could be a long wait, however, because bucks are not very active at this stage of the rut.

Close study of rubs may give you additional clues in how to hunt the buck that made them. Is the rub on only one side of the tree? Does it face a likely bedding area or a feeding area? If it faces the bedding area, it was probably made in the evening as the buck traveled toward his nighttime food supply. This may indicate the buck's favorite evening travel route, and a good place for an evening stand.

You may also find small scrapes beginning to appear as early as September. These platter-sized areas pawed free of leaves and sticks should not to be confused with the doe-attracting scrapes made later in the season. Like rubs, these scrapes serve as territorial markers and "practice" for the coming breeding season. Early scrapes rarely contain the bucks' saliva and tarsal-gland scent used later to attract does.

Initiation of Breeding Stage

As does begin coming into heat, buck activity takes a sharp increase. Hormone levels reach their peak in bucks during this stage (usually the last half of October) and bucks reach their peak aggressiveness. Violent fights among bucks occasionally take place this time of year. Does greatly increase their activity, a natural phenomenon that ensures they will expose themselves to breeding bucks.

While bucks are still establishing their order of dominance, some deer are beginning to breed. Bucks chase does that are not ready to breed, scenting the estrogen (female hormone) in their urine. Bucks range farther looking for the first does receptive to breeding and make many scrapes advertising stud service. When a doe is ready to breed, she may loiter at a scrape waiting for the buck to return.

Scrapes are of most importance to hunters at this time of the season, since bucks often (not always) visit them regularly to see if an eager doe has been there.

Things to remember about scrapes are that there is usually a primary scrape in the center of a line or circle of smaller scrapes. The primary scrape is the one the buck is most likely to visit,

Photo by Leonard Lee Rue III

As the hormone levels of whitetails peak in late October, bucks clash in an effort to establish dominance. Most disputes are settled by mild sparring; all-out fights occur only among equally mature and aggressive bucks.

167

Photo by Leonard Lee Rue III

Deer are attracted to the sound of a fight; does come to get acquainted with the victor, and big bucks want to know who is fighting in their neighborhood. Some hunters use this to their advantage to "rattle" deer to their stand.

normally checking it from downwind for the scent of other deer—or danger. Stands should thus be made downwind of the scrape 20–50 yards or so, depending on cover and whether you're hunting with gun or bow.

Primary and most secondary scrapes contain a wide range of sight and scent communication from the buck that made them. The area may be pawed in a wide circle (usually three feet in diameter); the buck has urinated into the scrape over his tarsal (hock) glands, leaving the scent of each. There is nearly always an overhanging branch the buck has chewed and rubbed with his face, leaving scent from his saliva, preorbital glands, and forehead glands. There may be a rubbed sapling and a concentration of feces at the site.

This stage is a time of very high activity among bucks and does. Simply spending a lot of time on a stand overlooking good whitetail travel routes should get you close to deer. The frenzy of deer behavior also gives the hunter a chance to use some creative tactics and have his best chance of taking a buck one-on-one.

Genuine breeding scrapes, made by bucks to attract does in heat, contain a large amount of buck scent and are checked regularly. This buck has left scent from facial glands on the overhanging branch, and is now urinating over his tarsal glands into the scrape.

Man-Made Scrapes

Fake scrapes can work any time of the rut, but are most effective early. Later, during the peak of the rut, there may be dozens of scrapes in an area, with the deers' attention divided among them. But if you make the first major scrape in the area, just as whitetails are getting into the breeding mood, you may attract special interest from the local deer herd. Another advantage of making your own scrape is that you can position it at a perfect stand location.

The purpose of making your own scrape is to lure the buck

to your stand. Theoretically he will come looking to confront a rival buck, or to contact does that are interested in breeding.

It is tricky business for a man to simulate the biological activity of a whitetail. If you want a buck to believe your scrape was made by another buck, you have to use the greatest care and genuine materials.

Start by making the scrape where you find signs of old scrapes (it is best to locate these sites during the previous season). If you make your scrape at the site of an old scrape, and the buck that made that old scrape is still around, chances are good that he is dominant and will come looking for the intruder.

Wearing clean rubber boots and gloves, and taking all other precautions to keep your scent off the surroundings, begin making the scrape. Use a stick to scratch out an area beneath an overhanging limb four or five feet off the ground, or set up your own overhanging branch. Scrape away all the vegetation on the ground until you have a circle of bare earth about three feet across.

For the first few days your scrape should have only the scent of a buck. This scent, primarily from urine, tarsal glands, and interdigital (hoof) glands, is available commercially in liquid form, or you may use actual uncontaminated hock glands from a dead buck. Place about 15 drops of liquid scent in the center of the

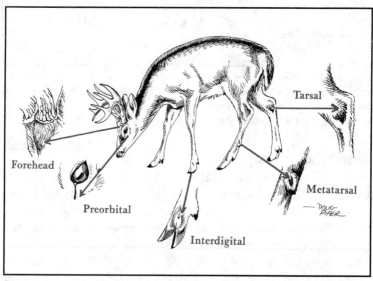

Scent communication among whitetails is most important during the rut. Both bucks and does interact through scent messages from urine and the glands shown above.

scrape, or drop the hock gland on the scrape and pound it into the soil. This may be sufficient to lure bucks to your stand. For utmost realism you may apply saliva and preorbital scent, taken from a dead buck, to the overhanging branch.

This scent should draw local bucks investigating the "intruder." Hunters and researchers have reported a variety of reactions among these bucks; very young bucks that have been beaten up in fights may shy away. Dominant bucks usually lay claim to the scrape, enlarging it and leaving scent on surrounding trees and ground, sometimes tearing up the area in a rage.

Photo by Mike Strandlund

Buck scent, as well as estrous doe scent, can be used to attract whitetails during the rut. Spray bottles let you direct strong charges of scent into the air.

If your initial scrape gets no response, or if activity subsides before you get your buck, you may add doe estrus urine to the scrape. This attracts bucks looking for does to breed.

Fake scrapes should be freshened with scent each day as you arrive at your stand. If the scrape is being visited but you are not seeing deer, bucks may be arriving at night. You can check this with a Trail Timer, a battery-operated device that records the time it was tripped by an animal. In cases of strictly nocturnal visitation, you may want to try another area that may have a buck active in daytime. Don't try to operate several fake scrapes in the same area, or your other scrapes will serve as competition for the one you are watching.

Rattling

Another aggressive technique for hunting the rut is rattling. As the breeding season starts, whitetail bucks that can't be intimidated by others begin to lock horns and wrestle to determine their hierarchy. As the rut progresses, these shoving matches get more severe, and may become quite violent between equally matched, superior bucks.

These battles attract the curiosity of other deer, especially larger, mature bucks that take exception to other bucks fighting for what they believe is their territory. For this reason, hunters who simulate buck fights by banging antlers together can often lure deer.

Since all deer antlers are different and sound different in a fight, just about any type of deer rack may be used in rattling. Shed or sawed-off antlers, natural or synthetic, may be used. In many cases it is better to have a larger-sized rack with long tines for best volume. Many hunters saw off the brow tines of their rattling antlers to prevent injuring their hands.

The method of rattling depends on the season and the circumstances. In the early stages, when bucks are merely sparring, it is more natural to rattle gently. Just tick the tines of the antlers together, scraping them occasionally.

After deer sign shows the rut is in full swing, louder, more violent rattling is in order. Bang the main beams together, rattle the tines, and grind the antlers together to simulate a shoving match. Pushing the racks together, tear them suddenly apart to sound like bucks separating. This type of rattling gets deer more excited and, because of its volume, attracts deer from a wider area.

While fighting is most common early in the rut, bucks may face off well into the later stages. Rattling may get results during any of these times.

Bucks do not fight in any particular pattern, so it is not necessary to conform to any certain rattling sequence. Most experienced rattlers recommend short rattling intervals of 30 seconds or so. If you rattle for long periods, a buck, approaching unseen, could pinpoint you while you're still rattling. A common technique is to rattle for 30- to 45-second periods with intervals of two to five minutes in which you wait, scanning the area, with your gun or bow in hand. Sometimes a fired-up buck will come charging, but usually they approach gingerly, scrutinizing the area, very suspicious because they know they should be able to see the noisy deer.

A rattling sequence will be more realistic if you use deer scent and stomp the ground to simulate the sound of deer hooves, and thrash bushes as if the deer are doing so with their antlers or bodies. These simulate the other elements of a buck battle.

More important than the antlers you use, or the way you use them, is setting up carefully. It is impossible to rattle in a buck that has seen, heard, or scented you. You won't get a shot unless you're in a position that lets you see deer and get a bullet or arrow through. It's best to know the area you are to hunt, and have an idea where the deer are, where you can set up, and how you can get there undetected.

Some hunters rattle deer from a tree stand, but this makes

a hunter very vulnerable to being spotted before he can get a shot. An effective tactic is for the rattler to remain hidden in a ground blind while a partner, the shooter, sits still in a tree stand downwind of the rattler.

Archers who rattle usually wear full camouflage to hide from the bucks' prying eyes. During the firearms season, however, it is imperative to wear full blaze orange because rattling can attract hunters, too.

Deer Calling

Deer calling, once considered a useless gimmick, is becoming popular as hunters realize it *is* possible to call deer. Deer calls include grunts, bleats, and snorts.

The grunt call is the most-used deer call. It simulates the moan-

Photo by Bill Bynum

Use of calls to attract deer is increasing among hunters. The most common is the grunt call, which simulates a rutting buck on the trail of a doe in heat.

ing sound a buck makes when he is trailing a doe in heat. Bucks may also grunt when they encounter each other. Some hunters have had success grunting with their voices, but most deer callers use commercial calls.

The grunt call probably attracts bucks because they think another buck is tending a doe in their territory. To grunt deer, set up near a scrape line and make a low, moaning sound lasting one to three seconds. The doe-tending grunt sounds somewhat like the grunt of a pig, but is monotone and drawn out. Make the call two or three times, then wait at least 15 minutes before calling again. All deer calling should be discreet.

The fawn bleat call is the oldest manufactured deer call. It is used to attract does, but some hunters report attracting bucks with a bleat.

Recent research shows that a well-made snort call may also attract deer. Commonly considered an alarm call, the snort may mean several other things. A short, loud snort usually signifies alarm, but a deer may use a drawn-out snort as a means of attracting the attention of other deer, perhaps to warn of perceived danger. Deer are put on alert, but may respond by carefully approaching the source of the sound.

Calls do not lure deer from very far. They are most effective to persuade a deer you have sighted to come close enough for a shot.

Several manufacturers make commercial deer calls, many of which work if properly used. Video and audio tapes from a reputable maker can help you hunt deer through the use of calls.

Some hunters occasionally blow a deer call as they rattle, which adds more authenticity to rattling. Common vocalizations among antagonistic bucks are the snort, wheeze, and grunt. A short snort is often followed by a wheezing, deep breath. The grunt, not to be confused with the doe-tending grunt, is much more brief and guttural.

Peak Breeding Stage

Three or four weeks after the first does begin coming into heat comes the peak of the rutting season—when the majority of the breeding deer are engaged in that activity.

During this phase of the rut, breeding bucks spend much of the day searching for does in heat. These far-ranging travels increase the probability of bucks wandering past a hunter's stand. On the other hand, bucks are unpredictable. They typically roam their territory until they encounter the scent of a doe ready to be bred. They then scent-trail the doe, hoping to find her in a receptive mood. The hunter can use this behavior to his advantage.

Scent Trails

One popular tactic this time of the year is to lay your own scent trails. Wear high-top rubber boots and take all other precautions to hide your own scent. Attach a scent pad to your boot or tie a long, clean rag around your ankle. Apply a generous amount of high-quality doe-in-heat (estrus) scent to the blotter, and walk to your stand. Walk over deer trails, scrape lines, and other places a buck is likely to pass. Drag the scent past your stand, through an area that offers a good shooting opportunity, and leave the rag on the ground, away from your tree stand or blind.

Don't consider this a sure-fire tactic; you won't find bucks

Photo by Mike Strandlund

A good rut-hunting tactic is to lay a trail of doe-in-heat scent through the woods to your stand, using a pad or rag attached to your boot. On rare occasions it has led trophy bucks right up to the hunter.

following wherever you go. But this method works often enough that it is well worth using every time you hunt deer during the rut.

Post-Rut Stage

As soon as the whitetail rut peaks, it begins to decline. More than 80 percent of the available does are bred during the three weeks surrounding the peak. Deer activity then diminishes and scrapes go neglected.

Many deer hunting seasons begin after rutting activity decreases. But while it may seem like the rut is over, it is not. Does that were not successfully bred during their first 24-hour estrus cycle come back into heat a month later. Spotty breeding activity may continue for six or eight weeks after the rut's peak.

While rattling and scrape watching are less productive during this stage, fake scrapes, calling, and scent trails still get results.

By this time you should know the location of many scrapes in the area you hunt. Check them periodically for signs of being

Photo by Roy Decker

When most does are bred and the woods have been stirred up by hunters, deer activity decreases. Bucks still roam the forest well into winter looking for the last receptive does, however.

Photo by Murray T. Walton

Abandoning their normal discretion, rut-crazed bucks downplay their concern for personal safety—but usually not to this extent.

freshened by a deer; if you find one, hunt it, because chances are good a deer will soon return. You may try freshening scrapes yourself with buck scent and doe estrus urine.

Tips for Hunting the Rut

Hunting the whitetail rut involves a vast amount of subtle tactics and maneuvers in response to the many elements of the whitetail's behavior. Here are some more tips for hunting the rut:

- Remember that most bucks scent-check scrapes before coming in to freshen them. Set up your stand downwind of the scrape.
- An active scrape will have the scent of deer urine and musk. A very fresh scrape will have a strong odor. Judge the age of the scrape, keeping in mind that bucks revisit primary scrapes about every other day. Plan your hunting around that knowledge.
- Deer may visit scrapes any time of the day or night. Heavily hunted deer are likely to be mostly nocturnal. But under normal conditions, there are peak periods during the day when deer visit scrapes. Whitetail researchers have found these are around 8:30 to 10:30 in the morning and 3:30 to 5:30 in the afternoon. Surprising to many deer hunters, there also seems to be a peak around noon.

- Whenever you are rattling, calling, or hunting over a scrape, remember that wary deer will usually approach you from downwind. Pay most of your attention to the downwind area and do all you can to keep the deer from scenting you.

  It may be near-impossible for a lone bowhunter to lure a buck into range before he is scented. In this case, a buddy system is a good tactic. The rattler conceals himself well while the shooter sets up about 50 yards downwind. If all goes as planned, the buck will circle downwind of the rattler, walking into range of the shooter before he can scent the hunters.

- The effectiveness of special rut-hunting tactics like rattling and fake scrapes depend on two factors: the amount of human activity in the area, and the buck/doe ratio where you hunt. If the area is under heavy hunting pressure, deer become nocturnal, moving very little during hunting hours. They may also be more suspicious or wise to rut tactics. Also, bucks that have all the does they need will not go out of their way to find another, and especially will not fight for one.

- Monitor deer behavior as closely as possible to find out when the rut peaks. Then spend as much time as possible in the woods. Your chances of scoring are much better then than any other time of the deer season.

Part III
The Complete Whitetail Hunter

Chapter 10

Perspectives on Whitetail Hunting

Whitetail hunting means something special, something different, to each hunter. For one, it is an annual ritual of putting wild meat on the table. For another, it is the challenge of hunting one certain trophy buck. For yet another, the best part of hunting is the camaraderie of deer camp.

There are many perspectives on whitetail deer hunting. Here are a few.

Advanced Whitetail Hunting

A true whitetail hunter does not hunt just for the kill, or for recognition among his peers, or even for achievement and recreation. In seeking the whitetail, a hunter actually seeks something else. The hunter is drawn to the outdoors and the animal and the hunt itself. There is an intellectual curiosity about nature. There is a fascination with the animal — its behavior and beauty. There is an undeniable yearning for the hunt, to become a skilled and knowledgeable deerstalker.

True hunters constantly learn and set new goals throughout their lives. Typically, they begin their hunting careers poking through woods close to home. At first the taking of any deer is a reasonable goal. But then they broaden their horizons. They range far to hunt, seeking bigger bucks and more challenging ways to hunt them. They spend more and more time hunting, knowing that while both good luck and bad luck play a part, in the final analysis you only get as much out of hunting as you put in.

What is a Trophy Hunter?

Many people, even some hunters, have misconceptions about trophy hunters. Some people picture a man after "braggin'-size horns," who cares little for the hunt and nothing for the game.

Photo by Wade Bourne

Deer hunting means something different to every hunter. The attraction may lie in the challenge of bagging a big buck, the camaraderie of deer camp, or in just "getting out."

Photo by Joe Workosky

Photo by Gerald Almy

Trophy hunters take on the test of limiting themselves only to the wisest, most mature bucks. An impressive rack symbolizes accomplishment of their hunting goals.

Actually, trophy hunters are among the most sincere hunters. They refine their skills to the utmost and make a commitment to go home empty-handed unless they meet a high level of challenge.

To the trophy hunter, an admirable set of antlers is a symbol he has achieved his personal hunting goal. There are no universal standards for trophies—each hunter makes his own definition. But there are constants; a trophy whitetail is a big-antlered buck, one that is smarter or more inaccessible than the common whitetail. Trophy hunting therefore requires a different approach than regular hunting.

The Elusive Trophy Whitetail

The world of trophy big game hunting generally agrees that the trophy whitetail hunter has the most difficult job of any hunter. No game is a greater challenge to hunt, and none has more competition among fellow hunters. Consider this: If you have $5,000 or more, you can fly to Alaska and hunt Dall sheep, spotting and stalking the animal you want, with comparatively little competition in the record book. But when you hunt whitetail bucks, you have competition from many other hunters. You have to "go in blind" and get very close. To get a whitetail trophy for the record book you not only compete against the wariest big game animal on the continent, but against millions of other hunters past and present.

Finding Big Bucks

If you're strictly after a trophy buck, the first consideration is finding a hunting area likely to hold trophy bucks.

Some hunters are willing to travel far for a chance at a big buck. They often wonder if there is a single part of the country that offers a better chance for a trophy whitetail. The answer is no. A look at the record books quickly reveals that the highest ranking heads in history have come from diverse backgrounds. For example, the top 10 nontypical trophies in Boone and Crockett come from four different regions. If you go down the list, you'll find bucks from every part of the country.

There are, however, some areas that stand out. The Great Lakes region—Minnesota, Wisconsin, Michigan, Illinois, and Iowa—has the biggest piece of the pie. Texas, with its small-bodied

Photo by Richard P. Smith

The trophy hunter's first task is finding mature bucks. While big-racked whitetails can be found in every state and province of the deer's range, the Great Lakes region and the Middle South are best represented in the record books.

but wide-antlered bucks, is also well represented. Considering the comparative hunting pressure, bucks from the far northern reaches of the whitetail range, including Alberta and Saskatchewan, may have most of the biggest bucks.

If you're planning on hunting close to home, it's best to consider whitetail pockets when trying to pin down those good isolated hunting spots for big bucks. Within each state are certain areas that offer the best chance for trophy whitetails.

Trophies Close to Home

Very smart bucks occasionally live several years in areas of high hunting pressure, but it is rare. In most areas, game managers

Photo by John Weiss

You may not have to go far to find a wall-hanger. Nearby woodlots may harbor big bucks that you can scout and hunt for as long as it takes.

estimate that 75 percent or more of the whitetail bucks are taken when they are 1½ years old. Only 1 percent or so of the deer herd may be bucks 4½ years or older—the age most bucks reach their trophy potential.

If there is a prime buck living in a heavily hunted area, it may be well known among hunters. You may be able to seek out the artful dodger and hunt him exclusively for the ultimate challenge in whitetail hunting. But remember, he's gotten old by playing the game right, and each year he gets smarter. For a chance of success, you may have to hunt him with binoculars for months in advance of the hunting season.

Wilderness Whitetails

There's a better chance of finding a trophy buck in areas of light hunting pressure. This usually means a large section of wilderness or an otherwise inaccessible area. These places aren't hunted as hard because they usually have fewer deer and are farther from population centers, and fewer hunters are willing to travel far into the bush in search of whitetails.

While deer are fewer in big-woods regions than in the farmlands, a much smaller percentage of the available bucks are taken each season, so the average age of bucks is higher. It's tougher to take a buck, but chances are better that the one you get will have a good rack.

Photo by Jim Churchill

A wilderness tent camp can give you access to areas of little hunting pressure. Here, bucks grow old and you can hunt in solitude.

Old wilderness bucks may be somewhat less wise to the ways of hunters than their ag-area counterparts. But because there are fewer hunters to keep deer moving, you need a more active approach to hunting. Scout hard for an optimum morning or evening stand, hone your still-hunting skills, or put on drives on manageable pieces of real estate.

Photo by Joe Workosky

Guided hunts from camps in prime whitetail areas yield high success rates and big bucks. Get references and plan ahead before booking a guided hunt.

Guided Hunts

For the hunter with limited time, the best chance at a trophy whitetail may be on a guided hunt. Outfitters base their operations in areas of superb deer hunting; they know where the big bucks are and how to get them.

Selecting a guide is a tricky business. The best way is to make an initial contact with a guide, get reliable references, and then have a good long discussion with the guide so you know exactly what you're getting. Some whitetail outfitters have several guides that conduct deer drives or help hunters spot and stalk deer. Others have well-positioned stands, while others simply provide a hunting area and turn the client loose.

Find out the type of hunting you'll do, what the guide will provide, and all other details. Your contacts will give you an idea of the guide's professionalism and concern for your needs. If you outline your plans and responsibilities through correspondence, it can serve as a simple contract.

You can obtain the addresses of whitetail guides through magazine and newspaper ads, through local chambers of commerce, and through the NRA Hunter Services Division's Hunter Information Service at NRA Headquarters.

Antlerless Deer Hunting

To many hunters, the antithesis of trophy hunting is antlerless deer hunting. Hunters can be a conservative lot, slow to accept changes or a change of mind. That's why many continue to resist antlerless deer hunting, steadfast in the belief that it harms deer herds and deer hunting, and is an unethical, unsportsmanlike practice.

Wildlife managers have proven time and again the importance of taking does as well as bucks. If does are not taken by hunters, they are doomed to eventual waste as a natural resource. In the many areas today where the deer population has saturated the habitat's carrying capacity, doe hunting is the best way to check the herd growth and prevent the overpopulation that can harm

Photo Courtesy U.S. Forest Service

Does are much more plentiful than bucks and less wary, which allows the antlerless deer hunter the best chance for success. Doe hunting is necessary for optimum whitetail management.

the area's entire deer herd. And doe hunting gives many hunters their only chance of success in a particular season.

Many hunters find little reward in a set of deer antlers. They find more satisfaction in the ritual of bringing home the venison, and want the best chance of doing so. For these hunters, antlerless deer hunting is their best shot at success.

State game departments all have different ways of conducting antlerless deer hunts. Some have permit systems coinciding with buck season; some are separate seasons; some allow a single antlerless permit for a hunting party.

Hunting strategies for doe hunters vary little from those of buck hunters. In areas of high deer concentration, simple trail watching will likely pay off for the patient hunter. Well-executed drives are a good bet later in the season when deer aren't moving.

Deer Camp

An inherent part of Americana, deer camp represents a vitally sought retreat from modern living, a way for many hunters to get in touch with old friends and an old way of life. For many, the annual days in deer camp serve to recharge the spirit and provide relief from the drudgeries of jobs and modern lifestyles.

An established deer camp is steeped in tradition, with long-standing members and its own set of rituals and customs. The camp's members have their traditional stands, traditional bunks, and traditional camp chores. Its quaint features are the woodstove and kindling pile, the outhouse, the dinner/poker/conference table, and the meat pole.

Typically, the permanent camp is a tin or tarpaper shack on land of little value to anyone except the hunter, and to him it is priceless. Deer camps may be built on leased hunting land, on a large parcel owned by the camp, or on a small parcel adjacent to public hunting ground.

Tent and trailer camps are more common. Usually on public land, their advantages are portability and low expense, giving hunters the freedom to hunt many different places. Though they lack the traditional aspects, their mobility and low cost in terms of time and money match the preferences of many deer hunters.

The camaraderie of deer camp cannot be denied; studies have shown that for the majority of deer hunters, the social element of the hunt is more important than any other.

Photo by State Historical Society of Wisconsin

Photo by Jim Hower

Yesterday and today, deer camp has been a way of escaping civilization and getting back in touch with close friends. Studies show that the companionship deer hunting provides is the most important element of the sport for most whitetail hunters.

CHAPTER 11

WHITETAILS ACROSS THE CONTINENT

O ur most adaptable big game animal, the whitetail deer is actually many different deer. Whitetails thrive from the cold and snow of Manitoba to the arid heat of Old Mexico. They're found in remote mountains and the backyards of suburbia; the Florida Everglades and Arizona desert. They'll run or hide or sneak, whatever they need to get them by.

For the best success, hunters should be just as adaptable, modifying their hunting approach to match the place they hunt.

Photo by Joe Workosky

Whitetails in the snow belt are the biggest bodied, often with antlers to match. Their large size is a biological adaptation that helps conserve body heat.

Snow Belt Whitetails

Northern whitetails, from Maine to the Dakotas, are known for their wide range and large size. The Upper Midwest has produced more record-book trophies than any other region, and the states of Wisconsin and Michigan have each yielded nearly a quarter-million deer annually in recent years. Hunters in Nebraska and the Dakotas, in gun seasons of only nine or 10 days, average better than 50-percent hunter success — over 75 percent in South Dakota.

Whitetails that live in the Northeast and Great Lakes Region fall into one of two categories: forest deer or farmland deer. The habitat, population dynamics, and hunting methods vary considerably between these environs.

The northern forest region extends about 100 miles south of the Canadian border. This region receives comparatively light hunting pressure and bucks are older on the average. Heavy winterkill, from long periods of deep snow and subzero temperatures, limits deer populations. Hunters who ply these woods for its whitetails have a poorer chance of getting a buck, but a better chance of getting a big buck.

South of the northern forest lies a region of farmland. Vir-

Photo by Leonard Lee Rue III

"Good tracking snow" is a boon to the northern deer hunter. It helps him find whitetails before and after the shot.

tually devoid of deer in the early 1900s, a whitetail population boom here has now threatened to exceed the land's carrying capacity. Deer hunting regulations have been liberalized in many northern farmland areas to curb the whitetail's population growth.

Still-hunting was for many years the traditional way of hunting north woods whitetails. Trail-watching and driving have become more popular in the last couple decades. The typical presence of snow is usually a blessing to the hunter, helping him track deer before and after the shot. Hard snowfalls and bitterly low temperatures can hamper the hunter, though, and weather in this region helps determine the season harvest. The occasional subzero temperatures and blizzard conditions during deer season keep both hunters and deer in their beds.

Due to the popularity of deer hunting here, there are usually plenty of hunters to keep deer moving in the northern farm areas. Wildlife managers have reported up to 40 hunters per square mile in some of the more popular areas. Hunting from blinds or tree stands is best during this time; after pressure eases several days into the season, driving is most productive.

In the big-woods region across the northern tier of states, hunting from long-established deer camps is common. In the more populated farm areas of the north, where deer are plentiful and usually close to home, hunters usually take day trips.

Midwest and Mideast Whitetails

Whitetails across the country's midsection enjoy milder weather, better food, and higher reproduction rates than their northern neighbors. The longer growing season helps bucks sprout impressive antlers: the highest-scoring Boone & Crockett Club whitetail was discovered in agricultural St. Louis County, Missouri. The main obstacle facing farmbelt whitetails is the loss of habitat resulting from urbanization and clean farming methods.

Photo by Stan Warren

Whitetail hunters in America's midsection set their sights on large deer herds and big bucks. Most of the highest-scoring whitetail trophies have come from the Midwest.

193

Photo by Richard P. Smith

Farmland deer are generally bigger and grow bigger antlers at a younger age than wilderness whitetails. While deer in mountains and big woods may have only spikes or forks at 1 ½ years of age, their corn-fed cousins often sprout six or eight points in their first rack.

Deer harvest rates are fairly low in many of these agricultural states considering the ample deer populations. This is due to relatively short hunting seasons and restrictions on firearms. In most of the open agricultural areas, centerfire rifles and handguns are generally prohibited; hunters must use shotguns or muzzleloaders.

Hunters in these agricultural areas do have some advantages, however. Forests are fairly sparse, so when corn is harvested, cover is greatly restricted. Deer become concentrated and easier to find.

In general, the more rural areas of the central states have ample public hunting areas, while the more populated areas have few. Agricultural areas usually support more deer per square mile of habitat than big-woods areas, and the farmland deer are usually bigger in body and antler.

Deer Down in Dixie

While deer hunting usually conjures up images of snowy November woods, it comes as a surprise to many northerners that some of the best deer hunting in the country is in the Deep South. Notable examples are Alabama and Mississippi, where bag limits are basically a deer a day for a two-month gun season.

While southern deer are abundant, they do not normally reach the trophy dimensions of their northern cousins. Whitetails, like all mammals, are bigger in body in their ranges farthest from the equator. Their antlers generally follow suit. A distinct exception to this is the small-bodied, big-racked Texas whitetail.

Southern deer seasons begin in August or September, when oppressive heat can make hunting uncomfortable and carcass-handling tricky. The heat can be used to the hunter's advantage,

Photo by Gerald Almy

Predominantly rural with a lush growing season, the Deep South harbors some of the largest whitetail populations. Seasons and bag limits are liberal.

however. The combination of high temperatures and low water supplies in many parts of the South concentrate deer in the areas of available water. Locating the primary water sources near feeding and bedding areas will mean locating a lot of deer.

Other considerations for warm-weather southern hunters are the presence of poisonous snakes and biting insects. Insect repellent or a headnet, and snake-proof boots or chaps, are a good idea.

While still-hunting and stands are popular among deer hunters everywhere, southern deer hunters have traditionally used a few other methods. They make more use of tree stands, and occasionally use hounds and buckshot, which are illegal in many other

Photo by Bill Bynum

In hot, dry times, the southern deer hunter looks for scarce sources of water to find whitetail concentrations.

parts of the country. Antler rattling, which originated in Texas, has always been most popular south of the Mason/Dixon Line. Swamp buggies and tight drives are best for hunting the elusive coastal marsh whitetails.

Western Whitetails

Most hunters think of mule deer and the bigger big game species when they think of the West. Actually, the western states and provinces offer excellent whitetail hunting that is getting even better as whitetails expand their range west. Many of the largest whitetails ever taken have come from areas often considered too far west for good whitetail hunting.

There are four important subspecies of whitetails that live in the West. They include the Texas, Coues, Dakota, and Northwest subspecies.

The Texas whitetail, which is almost entirely confined to its namesake, is a populous subspecies. There are almost 4 million whitetails in Texas. With few exceptions, most hunting here is on private land leased to organizations or groups of hunters. It

Photos by Bob Gooch

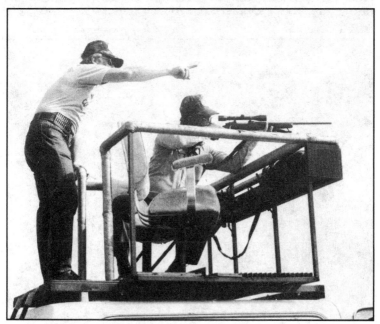

Horses, hounds, and truck-top shooting platforms are common on whitetail hunts in some southern areas.

197

follows that the best leases are the most expensive. Trophy hunters know that the southern part of the state gives up the most wallhangers.

Because Texas brush is dense at ground level, much of the hunting is from elevated stands, which allow greater visibility from above the thick vegetation. These are usually permanent stands made of metal or wood strategically placed along typical travel routes. Serious hunters in very brushy areas make *senderos*, which are wide swaths cut through the brush for the purpose of seeing and shooting deer in thickets.

Other popular techniques for Texas whitetails are hunting from vehicles and over bait. While these methods are illegal in many states, Texas wildlife officers say their deer populations must be cropped heavily to achieve the desired harvest, and baiting and road hunting prove to be effective deer management methods.

The Coues (pronounced "cows") is a diminutive whitetail, much smaller than other western subspecies. Coues deer dwell in Arizona and Mexico, and there is also a small population in New Mexico.

Most Arizona hunters favor the bigger resident mule deer, but there is a growing interest in the Coues, which lives primarily in the arid, rocky southern part of the state.

Photo by Gerald Almy

With a herd of 4 million whitetails — many of them wide-antlered bucks — Texas is one of America's finest deer-hunting states.

The small Coues whitetail is a tough quarry, finding refuge among the cactus and rubble of the rugged, arid mountains of the Southwest.

This is a very wary deer, well-known for hiding and holding its ground when hunters approach. A popular hunting technique is to glass carefully in the morning when deer are moving. In areas of sparse vegetation, you can often spot upwards of a dozen deer. Follow their movements carefully until you see them bed down; then start a stalk using wind direction, topography, and vegetation to your advantage.

Coues deer country is usually rough, with plenty of rocks and steep terrain. The weather is apt to be hot, so plan accordingly. Wear rugged boots, carry plenty of water, and make arrangements for hot-weather meat-handling.

The Dakota whitetail lives in the Upper Midwest, the eastern Rocky Mountain states, and Canada's prairie provinces. This whitetail subspecies accounts for a good share of record-book heads, with most of them from Montana, Alberta, and Saskatchewan.

Farmland fringes, brushy creekbottoms, and forested river

Photo by Mike Strandlund

Hunters in the far West have recently come to enjoy the hunting opportunities offered by a new resident game animal—the whitetail.

valleys are the prime habitats for this whitetail. In Montana, for example, the Yellowstone and Missouri Rivers provide excellent environments for whitetails. Cottonwood forests underlain with willow and other shrubs are ideal bedding areas, while adjacent farmlands in the fertile riverbottoms provide excellent forage. Colorado's South Platte is a well-known whitetail region, as are the Black Hills of Wyoming and South Dakota.

This region commonly sees large numbers of whitetails feeding in fields early and late in the day. Hunters take positions in tree stands or river bluffs before daylight, waiting for deer to return to cover. The reverse holds true in the afternoon, as deer leave cover and head for the croplands.

While mule deer hunts generally open in October, special whitetail seasons are often held during the month of November, giving hunters the advantage of pursuing whitetails during their breeding season.

The Northwest whitetail also seeks farmlands, but is very much at home in evergreen forests, sharing its range with elk. One of the biggest whitetails in the record book came from a heavily forested area in western Montana.

The whitetail is constantly expanding its range west, following river-bottoms and moving into woods, agricultural areas, even mountainsides with less-than-ideal habitat.

Many of the big bucks from here are taken incidentally by elk hunters who also have deer tags. Northeast Washington, northern Idaho, and all of northwest Montana produce large whitetails. The adaptive deer increases its range annually into Oregon and other western states.

Despite the presence of whitetails in Rocky Mountain states, the mule deer has traditionally been the preferred species among deer hunters. But those attitudes are changing as hunters discover the quality and increasing opportunities of western whitetail hunting.

Urban Whitetails

Throughout the country are cities and suburbs surrounded by deer-occupied farms and forests. More and more, whitetails are intermingling with these urban areas and offering close-to-home hunting opportunities for city folks.

The whitetail's unsurpassed senses, escape abilities, and adaptive temperament allow him to live very close to civilization. While most of us insist on traveling to hunt deer, we may be passing up bucks literally in our own backyards.

Deer that live close to humans tend to be either more wary or more passive than their wilderness counterparts. If the deer are hunted, they view each of their frequent encounters with humans as a hunting situation and take evasive measures. They learn much from these encounters, and become very difficult to catch flat-footed. Conversely, deer that have not been hunted, that have experienced no danger in their encounters with people, become less wary.

Deer that live in urban areas are often easier to pattern than wilderness whitetails. Their movements must often go through narrow strips of cover around yards, highways, developed areas, and other obstacles. Scout thoroughly, and you should be able to identify some bottlenecks of deer movement.

The biggest problem facing the urban hunter, of course, is people. Sometimes the everyday activities of people may destroy your plans; your favorite woodlot may be a housing development next year. Sometimes there may be too many other hunters competing for the same deer. But as mentioned, there are often deer habitats close to town that never see hunters, simply because they *are* so close to town. Suburban deer can get very old and large.

Photo by Mike Strandlund

The adaptive whitetail makes use of food and shelter wherever it finds it, even in the heart of civilization. Increasing numbers of "downtown deer" have created a nuisance in some areas.

Range of the Whitetail

The whitetail deer has expanded its range considerably in recent decades, the result of improved habitat, good management, and increased adaptability. Some biologists believe there are more whitetails now than in pre-Columbian times.

The whitetail may occupy just about any type of habitat found in North America, and there are many big differences between subspecies. But there are also constants, including the deer's attraction to agricultural, edge, and wetland corridor areas. Find these, no matter where you are, and that's where you're most likely to find the whitetail.

203

CHAPTER 12

TRAILING AND RECOVERING DEER

The truest test of a hunter's woodsmanship comes after the shot, when he may have to follow a difficult trail to recover his deer.

First there's only a thin line of alders separating the cedar thicket from chest-high marsh grass, small openings indicating deer paths crossing before your blind.

Then suddenly there's the flick of an ear, then the shake of a tail. A leg seems to materialize as it takes a tentative step forward. And a whitetail buck appears like the evening fog.

Your rifle arrives unbeckoned to your shoulder. With confidence built on hours and ammo spent at the range, you settle the crosshairs. The silence is shattered and the scene blurs, and you know it was a good shot even as the gun recoils. But when it comes back down, you can only gawk at the buck dashing across the swamp and into the far trees.

What happened? How could you have missed?

First of all, calm down. An excited hunter is a hunter who makes mistakes. Chances are the buck is yours if you know what to do and have the discipline to do it right.

The shot, with either gun or bow, may be the end of a deer hunt. The hunter walks up to his or her prize, admires it, tags and dresses it, and drags it out. The hunt is over.

But in many cases, there's another step after the shot that can be the most important element of the hunt: trailing and recovering wounded game.

Did You Miss?

The first step in recovering wounded deer is establishing whether the shot hit the deer. This step should be approached subjectively; you should *always assume the deer was hit* unless an exhaustive investigation proves otherwise.

When bowhunting, you can often see if the arrow strikes the deer, but don't be fooled. An arrow may appear to miss when it really didn't. There may be no reaction from a hit deer. If the arrow strikes the deer, you should be able to hear it. Another good sign, but also a tricky one, is the behavior of the deer immediately after the shot. Deer usually flinch, kick their hind legs, and jump into the air when hit, and almost always break into a dead run with their tail down. If the deer stands there looking around and pivoting its ears, you missed and the deer is trying to figure out where you are before it runs. If it runs off deliberately, tail up, you probably missed and the deer knows who you are, where you are, and what you want. But don't depend on this refutable evidence.

A deer shot in the neck or lungs may run as if it has an in-

A whitetail's behavior may give clues to how well the shot was placed. Unscathed whitetails usually bound with tail up, while wounded deer dash with tail down—though these rules don't always hold true.

jured front leg. A heart-shot deer dashes off hard and straight, but you may hear it fall. A deer hit in the paunch usually humps up, arching its back. A deer shot in a rear leg or hip may so indicate by the way it runs.

The deer's mental condition plays a part in the amount of trailing required. If the deer is calm, a solid hit may drop it in its tracks. But if it is nervous with adrenaline flowing, such as on a drive-hunt, the same shot may send it on a long run before it runs out of gas.

Always stay alert when taking a shot at a whitetail on the chance you may have to follow it. You want to confirm if and where the deer was hit. Be prepared to take a second shot, even if the deer goes straight down. Hunters have lost "dead" deer that caught them off guard and got back up to dash off. If you can, take as many more shots as are safe and reasonable. They could make the difference in whether you recover the deer.

Assess the Situation

Don't go running off through the woods like a hound dog chasing the deer; stop a moment to think things over. Piece together the evidence and try to determine what exactly happened and what you should do.

Before leaving your stand, note the spot where the deer was shot, the spot where you last saw the deer, and its direction of travel at that moment. Listen carefully until it runs out of hearing distance, and mentally mark that approximate spot. The reason for noting all these things is that a deer may not leave a blood trail immediately; then it may leave only occasional drops of blood. Your best chance of recovering the deer may be going to the last spot you saw or heard it, then following a faint blood trail to the animal.

Photo by Mike Strandlund

A close examination of the place you shot your deer will reveal evidence as to where the deer was hit, how badly it was wounded, and which way it went.

Pick a marker such as a tree or bush near the place where you last saw the deer. Leave your stand and go there first, to make sure you don't lose track of that last spot where the deer was sighted. Look for blood, and whether or not you find some, mark the spot with a cap or other large, visible object.

Trail Immediately, or Wait?

The way you should proceed depends on several factors. In some cases hunters need to weigh the situation carefully to decide whether to follow immediately or to wait before trailing. Hunters should usually take an active approach to recovering an animal. Sometimes it's best to proceed passively, but not for the reason most hunters think. Deer do not "lie down and stiffen up" as many hunters believe; in fact, the wound begins to repair itself almost immediately. It is a matter of whether the deer succumbs to shock or blood loss before it fully recovers.

A deer's body has an amazing capacity to repair wounds and replace lost blood. If a deer keeps moving, the wound is less likely to close and the deer will lose more blood. Also, a deer's heart beats three times faster when it is moving than when it's still, which makes it bleed that much harder. A moving deer uses up more of its stored energy, making it weaker and less able to regenerate blood. Immediate blood-trailing is most important in warm weather; the carcass may begin to spoil in less than an hour.

There are several other reasons for following a deer immediately. The shock and tissue damage from a bullet may disable and/or disorient a deer quick enough and long enough for a hunter who follows immediately to get another crack at it. A good blood trail from a bullet means a solid hit, which means the animal also absorbed full shock from the bullet and is probably already dead. You must also be quick in trailing the wounded deer if rain or snow starts to obliterate the blood trail. The same holds true for very dry conditions, in which blood may dry quickly and be harder to see. In most areas, it is not advisable to dawdle in the recovery of a buck during gun season. If you don't tag it soon, someone else may.

If a bowhunter sees the arrow penetrate just behind the front leg, and has a waist-high blood trail on both sides of the path, there's no reason to wait. In such cases, deer bleed to death within 30 seconds. A rather faint blood trail means the deer was not badly injured and must be pushed if it is to lose enough blood and energy.

One exception to following a wounded whitetail immediately is if it has been wounded in the paunch, or guts. Follow the trail slowly until you determine the deer has traveled a considerable distance. Wait at least a couple hours, then trail quietly in case it is alive in its bed.

In some cases bowhunters should give their broadheads time to work. With a moderate blood trail, it may be best to wait. Arrowed whitetails may feel little pain or fright. They often travel only a short distance before laying down and bleeding to death. But if they sense a trailing hunter, they may panic and run fast and far, leaving a long, sparse blood trail that is easy to lose. Each situation must be considered individually.

Approaching darkness is not an excuse to delay; blood is easy to follow at night with a lantern or flashlight. Most fatally wounded whitetails are recovered within 200 yards of where they were shot. There are exceptions: Deer that have been driven or are otherwise excited can keep going longer through the effects of adrenaline. Paunch and liver wounds may allow whitetails to travel farther.

Photo by J. R. Lamson

Don't give up the trail because of darkness. A lantern gives blood drops a luminescent appearance and actually makes trailing easier at night.

Difficult Trailing Situations

You may find little or no blood at the point where the deer disappeared. Go to the spot where the deer was standing when you shot, and make a search. Look for blood, hair, chips of bone, and, if you were bowhunting, the arrow shaft. Look for blood both on the ground and on vegetation about two feet off the ground behind the spot where the deer was standing. These may provide valuable clues to the location and lethality of the hit.

Any shot that strikes a deer will cut hair and leave it at the point of the hit. If the hair is all the same length, and there is no blood, it usually means the shot was a grazing one — probably not lethal. If there is no blood but there are longer hairs *and* shorter ones, the bullet or arrow probably penetrated, but not completely. In either case, keep looking for blood.

Lighter brown hair comes from legs and midbody; longer, darker hair comes from the brisket and the back. Longer white hair comes from the belly or rump; shorter white hair may have come from the throat.

The appearance of the blood also indicates the location of a hit. Pink fluid full of tiny bubbles indicates a lung hit. Bright red blood comes from the heart, an artery, or capillaries in a muscle. Dark red blood comes from the liver or kidney, while watery blood mixed with food particles comes from the paunch.

For a bowhunter, the arrow shaft can reveal the most valuable clues. A shaft found on the spot of the hit, literally covered with pink or bright red blood, is the sign of a quickly fatal hit. There should be a very good blood trail. If the shaft is relatively clean, the hit was probably marginal. If it is covered with a greasy substance and has a strong odor, the hit was in the paunch.

The type of blood and hair can give you some idea of the location of the hit, but don't read too much into this sign. Hair length and color varies among deer. The blood may indicate where the bullet or arrow hit, but it may not indicate *all* that the projectile hit. For example, you may take a quartering-away shot, and find that the sign indicates a paunch hit. But the bullet may have also travelled into the lungs, where all the bleeding was internal.

Blood Trailing

When it's time to trail, go to the point closest to the animal where you found blood and begin following. When looking for blood, concentrate on the ground but keep an eye on tree trunks, leaves, and grass above ground level where some blood may have wiped off. Blood may also be sprayed to the sides of a trail.

On a sparse blood trail, mark each blood spot with a large, highly visible marker such as tissue or surveyor's flagging. It helps you backtrack when you lose the trail.

Trailing is easy in snow. Even very tiny drops of blood stand out. If the blood trail stops, you can still follow the tracks. Tracks of the deer you're after may mix with those of other deer. If so, look for a distinguishing feature of the track, such as an ingrown hoof or a dragging leg.

If there is very little blood and the ground is bare, trailing is best done on hands and knees. Tracking here is a case of search and search, find a tiny pinpoint of blood, and search again. Mark each drop of blood with a piece of tissue or similar material before looking for the next drop. Be very careful not to obliterate any blood sign as you look—walk to the side of the blood trail, not over it. You may be better off waiting till nightfall and trailing with a lantern. Drops of blood catch the light at night and are much easier to see.

A blood trail that starts out with significant, red blood but then peters out is often indicative of a nonfatal muscle wound. You should remain on the trail, however, in case there is internal bleeding. Continue following until you find where the deer bedded down. You'll find one of three things: The deer is dead; the deer lost much blood in its bed and is still bleeding; the deer lost little blood in its bed and will probably survive. At any rate, if you haven't found the deer, keep looking.

It is easy to lose a faint blood trail. When you do, mark the last blood and search in half-circles in the direction the deer was going. Also keep your eyes peeled for scuffed leaves, broken or bent plants, and tracks. Two or three hunters working together are often more effective at following a blood trail than one person, as long as they do it in organized fashion, searching thoroughly before walking through it and possibly covering blood sign. Sometimes one hunter can slowly follow the blood trail while another walks ahead, hoping to find blood closer to the game and save time. If you can't regain the blood trail, go back down the trail you've marked and search for blood on each side. A wounded animal will often double back on the path, then stagger off its course as it begins to lose consciousness.

Sometimes a deer will walk in circles and, on a forest floor with thick dead leaves, it may be difficult to tell which way it was going. Certain signs may tell you: Drops of blood may splatter in the direction that a deer was moving. If a whitetail was hit on the right side and there is no exit wound, blood will be present only on the right side of the trail in the direction the deer was going. If there is blood on both sides of the trail, but heavier on one side, the side with the heaviest blood sign is probably the side with the exit wound. Close examination of hoofprints in leaves or occasional bare spots may show the way the deer was headed.

Finding Deer When There's No Blood

If there is no blood trail at all but you're sure of a hit, there are other ways of recovering the animal. Go to the point where the deer vanished, take a compass reading on its flight line, and make a systematic search for at least 300 yards. Look for both blood and the deer itself. In thick cover, it may be difficult to see the deer even if you come quite close. You may be able to smell the deer if you can get within 15 yards or so downwind.

If you can't find the deer, stay at the scene or return after a few hours. Crows, magpies, ravens, and other scavenger birds may have the animal located, and tip you off with their calls. Vultures are silent, but may be easy to spot.

One of the best ways to find deer when there's no blood trail is with a tracking dog. Be sure it is legal in your state or county.

Here are some other tips on recovering wounded deer:

Don't hesitate to take a careful follow-up shot.

Wounded animals usually travel downhill and toward cover.

Deer wounded in the paunch usually head for water.

In open country or sparse woods, keep watch ahead with

binoculars. You may spot the wounded animal in its bed and be able to dispatch it without disturbing it further.

- As you trail, be careful about getting lost. It is very easy to do as you walk circles in the woods, watching the ground. This is another reason to mark the trail you follow.
- If you wound a deer but can't recover it, keep hunting that deer. Still-hunt through probable bedding sites in the area.

Trailing a wounded deer can take dedication and perseverance in the face of frustration, but the rewards are always worth the effort. There's a lot of satisfaction in successfully recovering a deer at the end of a difficult blood trail.

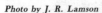
Photo by J. R. Lamson

In tough blood-tracking situations, persistence pays off. Even if the trail disappears, keep searching until you find the deer or exhaust any possibility of recovering the game.

Approaching a Wounded Deer

Always trail wounded deer quietly, in case they are alive and you may be able to sneak close for a shot.

Sometimes you may discover your deer down but still alive. Get close enough for a sure shot, but not too close—cause as little distress as possible. Shoot does in the head and bucks in the top of the neck. Even if you don't want to save the antlers, they may need to be intact for you to register and legally possess the animal.

Approach a downed deer cautiously, ready to take a shot. If the eye is open, unblinking, the deer is dead; if it is closed, a finishing shot will be necessary.

Most states have strict laws requiring that you carefully fill out and at-tach a carcass tag immediately after locating your deer.

If the deer appears dead, approach from behind — away from hooves and antlers — and check the eye. If the eye is closed, the deer is still alive and must be dispatched. If it is open, carefully lean forward and touch it with a stick. If there is no response, you can be sure the deer is dead.

Most states and provinces require you to tag the deer immediately at this point before you attempt to transport or field dress the carcass.

Field Dressing

The quality of your venison will depend on how quickly you dress out the deer and cool the meat. It should be done immediately with a sharp, strong-bladed knife. There are several variations of this procedure; here is one of the best:

If an incline is handy, position the deer with the head uphill and roll it onto its back. Stand over the rear of the deer, facing the head, keeping it on its back by leaning one of its legs against your leg.

Photo by Richard P. Smith

A careful, systematic approach to field dressing will save meat from spoilage and make the operation more pleasant.

With a buck, remove the sex organs first. Then make a small cut near the back legs to help you find the proper depth of the cut. You must cut through the hide and several layers of muscle and connective tissue, making sure you don't puncture the intestines. Cut through carefully, one layer at a time, until you see the gray folds of intestine. When you cut through, the intestines will tend to squeeze out through the cut.

If you are right-handed, place the first fingers of your left hand under the cut, palm upward and fingers pointing toward the deer's head. Carefully put your knife blade edge-up between your fingers. Pull up with your left hand, pulling the hide and tissues away from the intestines. Using your left hand as a guide, make a vertical cut up the center of the belly until you reach the sternum (bottom of the rib cage). Then remove your left hand and use both hands to cut most of the way through the sternum toward the neck. Cutting through the sternum requires considerable force, and you must be careful the knife doesn't slip. This procedure is easier if you cut along one side of the sternum. Don't make this cut if you are planning to have a shoulder mount made.

Finish slitting open the belly by cutting back toward the anus, again using your fingers to keep from cutting the intestines.

Let the carcass fall to one side, and the entrails will begin to roll out. Reach in on one side and pull them as far as they will easily come. You will have to carefully reach in and cut some connective tissue to get the entrails out entirely. Be careful not to cut yourself on your knife or on sharp pieces of broken bone. Avoid damaging the tenderloins — the two strips of muscle in the lower back lying parallel to the spine.

A thin membrane of muscle (the diaphragm) at the bottom of the rib cage must be cut away. This will give you access to the heart, lungs, and windpipe. Reach past the pink lungs until you can feel the tube-like windpipe near the throat. Grasping it, reach in with the knife and cut it free. Pull it out along with the heart and lungs.

Save the heart (it is fist-sized and hidden among membrane near the lungs) and the liver (the large, dense, dark-colored organ). Wipe away any dirt or other contamination, and put the heart and liver in a plastic bag if you wish to save them.

The final step is to cut completely around the anus to remove the lower digestive tract and bladder. This is easiest if you can split the arch of the pelvic bone with an axe or large knife, but it isn't necessary. Some hunters insert a stick in the anus and cut around the stick.

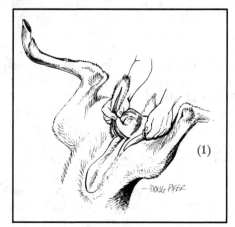

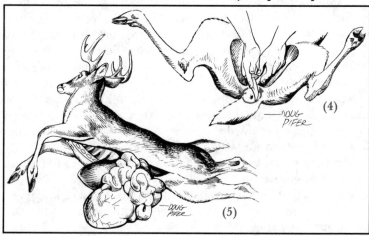

These are the steps in field-dressing a deer: (1) If your deer is a buck, remove the sex organs. Do not cut into the body cavity. (2) Cut through the belly skin without puncturing the intestines. With the sharp edge upturned, guide the knife with your fingers until you have cut through the belly hide. (3) Cut through the sternum. (4) Finish the belly cut to the anus, split the pelvis bone, and cut out the colon. (5) Turn the deer to one side and make any more cuts as necessary to spill the paunch.

Be careful not to spill urine from the bladder—a small, translucent sac. Some hunters tie off the tube between the kidney and bladder to keep urine from spilling. It's important to remove all fat and contaminating substances from the anus area. The meat in that area will quickly spoil otherwise.

If intestinal matter got on any part of the meat, wipe it off with leaves, snow, grass, paper, or cloth. Sometimes it's better to slice away the outer layer of contaminated meat.

Once it's cleaned, elevate the carcass to help it drain and cool. It can be propped against a rock, bush, or double tree trunk. Insects may be a problem in warmer weather; if so, keep the body cavity covered and get it to a cool place as quickly as possible.

If you plan to let the carcass hang for a few days, remove the tenderloins first; otherwise they may become hard and dry.

Here are some other points to remember in field-dressing whitetails:

Field dressing is messy and strenuous, so you may want to remove your blaze orange coat. If you do, hang it up nearby so it is visible to other hunters. Your movement, bent-over outline, presence of the deer, and unawareness of other hunters may create a dangerous situation. Keep a blaze orange hat on.

Do not cut the deer's throat. Dead deer do not bleed, so it is unnecessary and will just make more of a mess. Removing entrails will remove all the blood possible. If the deer is alive, it is dangerous to you and inhumane to the deer to cut its throat. It should be shot.

Do not try to remove tarsal (hock) glands of bucks. Some hunters perform this step under the theory that the gland may taint meat. But there is a better chance of that happening if it is cut or if scent is transferred by the knife blade to meat.

Taking Out the Carcass

Hopefully, you've made arrangements for getting the deer out of the woods and to a place where it can be butchered.

Dragging a deer out is preferably a two-man operation. An average man has difficulty dragging an average whitetail more than a half-mile or so. A big buck can be near impossible for a sole hunter to get out by himself.

For a two-man drag, each hunter can simply grab a front leg or an antler and pull. Some hunters prefer to drag with ropes

Photo by Gerald Almy

Photo by Richard P. Smith

The cumbersome chore of transporting a deer carcass from the woods has inspired many various approaches to the job. Deer are easiest to drag head forward, even easier with the help of an internal combustion engine.

Photo by John Weiss

or with a stick tied to the antlers or front legs. When dragging, try to keep the deer on its side and dirt out of the body cavity.

Dragging is much easier over snow than dry land. There are commercial aids to dragging such as big-wheeled carts and heavy-plastic sleds. They ease the dragging job but are seldom practical to take hunting.

For long-distance hauling, some hunters use the pole-carry method, with the deer hung on a long pole with ends carried over the shoulders of two hunters. This method can create more work than it saves, however, and may be dangerous. Some hunters carry small deer out on their shoulders. This is very dangerous and overly strenuous, however. If you do carry deer, mark the carcass with plenty of blaze orange material. Snowmobiles, all-terrain vehicles, and horses make hauling deer a breeze. Do so responsibly; don't make ruts or disturb other hunters.

CHAPTER 13
TROPHIES AND VENISON: FRUITS OF THE HUNT

Photo by Joe Workosky

A sharp, well-composed hunting photo is one of the best trophies a whitetail hunter can collect. You'll always be glad you took the time to take good pictures.

You've brought your buck down and out of the woods. Now is the time to enjoy the fruits of your hunt: the savory venison and memory-inspiring trophy.

Considerable time and skill go into this final phase of your hunt. There are several ways of preparing trophies and of skinning, butchering, and cooking venison. Many hunters have all the work done by a taxidermist and butcher, but there is a certain satisfaction in doing it yourself.

Capture Your Hunt on Film

Photographs of the hunt and those rare moments of success are among the hunter's favorite trophies.

If you want top-quality pictures or enlargements, a 35mm camera is a must. The newer autofocus cameras are a good choice, enabling amateur photographers to get very good pictures. They are convenient to carry and some have small, built-in flash systems for pictures in low light. Single-lens reflex (SLR) cameras can provide even better quality, but they are more bulky to carry and take more expertise to operate. If you get a camera with a self-timer, you can take photos of yourself when you're alone.

The best color enlargements come from slide film with a low ASA (light sensitivity) rating, such as Kodachrome 64. Higher ASA film such as 200 or 400 allows you to take pictures with less light, but quality diminishes. The same holds true for print film — the best choice if you want a large number of smaller prints for a photo album.

In taking pictures, do all you can for technical quality. Try to put your subject in good light without harsh shadows. Focus carefully, make sure your shutter speed is fast enough, take time to compose your pictures, and mind details. Set up the pictures for aesthetic appeal and include all elements important to the moment — you, your deer, the surroundings, friends, camp scenes, etc. Photos of dead deer should be taken tastefully; keep blood, wounds, and tongues out of the picture. It's best to take photos before field dressing the deer.

If you're interested in photographing whitetails (a great off-season activity), you'll need a high-quality camera, a telephoto lens of at least 200mm, and skills to use them well. Be ready for a challenge — getting a good shot with a camera is much harder than with a gun.

Trophy Ranking and Preparation

Antlers have held a fascination for hunters since time immemorial. Some of man's earliest cave drawings show antlers as a symbol of religion, bounty, and respect for nature. They still carry a deep meaning to modern hunters, so they are almost always preserved.

Considered by many to be a measure of a hunter's success, the size and formation of antlers receive a lot of attention. Hunters often like to rank good-sized racks to see how they compare to others.

Whitetail antlers fall into two basic categories: typical and nontypical. A typical rack is symmetrical with all its points jutting out above the main beam. A nontypical trophy may have gross deformities, points jutting out from other points, or points that jut downward from the main beam.

The NRA Hunter Recognition Program, operated by NRA Hunter Services Division, recognizes trophies taken by NRA members. Whitetails with at least four points on one side (three points for Coues) qualify for a personalized walnut plaque. Those exceeding Boone and Crocket Club minimums may be entered in the NRA Leatherstocking Award Contest. The program awards handsome statuettes to hunters who have taken the top-ranked big game animal of the year in categories of long gun,

Photo by Mike Strandlund

The fascinating configurations of whitetail antlers, and the stately image of a majestic buck's head, make cape mounts popular among trophy hunters.

225

If you have taken a very large whitetail trophy and think it may qualify, contact the Boone and Crockett Club for a list of official measurers in your geographical area. Official measurements cannot be taken until 60 days after the animal was taken, to allow for drying and shrinkage. Using an official scoring sheet this measurer is preparing to score this impressive whitetail for the Boone and Crockett Club Recordbook.

handgun, muzzleloader, and archery. Only NRA members may enter these programs.

Official entry forms and more information for the programs are available by writing to the NRA Hunter Recognition Program, National Rifle Association, 1600 Rhode Island Avenue, NW, Washington, DC 20036 (telephone 202-828-6240).

Very large racks may qualify for ranking in the *Records of North American Big Game*, a book published by the Boone and Crockett Club. Antlers are measured and one point is given for

The Boone and Crockett number-one nontypical whitetail rack is this one, taken from a road-killed buck found in Missouri in 1981. It scored 333⅞ points.

each inch in a variety of length and girth measurements. Trophies entered in the typical category are penalized for abnormalities or lack of symmetry. For official ranking, the measurements must be taken by an official B&C measurer at least 60 days after the deer was taken, to allow for shrinkage.

To qualify for ranking in the record book, a typical whitetail rack must score 160 points and a nontypical 185 points. There is a separate category for the Coues whitetail of the southwestern U.S.; the minimum scores for ranking a Coues are 100 and 105 points.

The current number-one Boone and Crockett whitetail head is a nontypical rack from a road-killed buck found in St. Louis County, Missouri, in 1981. It scored 333⅞ points. The number-one typical head was shot in Burnett County, Wisconsin, in 1914; it scored 206⅛ points. The top Coues deer, which scored 143 points, was taken in Pima County, Arizona, in 1953.

Boone and Crockett Club headquarters are located at 241 S.

Photo by William Nesbitt, Boone and Crockett Club

Scoring 206⅛ points, the B&C number-one typical whitetail head was shot in 1914 in northern Wisconsin.

Photo by Joe Workosky

A tape measure with a girth/weight formula lets you determine your buck's weight without a scale. The tape measures are available commercially.

Fraley Blvd., Dumfries, VA 22026 (telephone 703–221–1888).

Bowhunters may enter the above programs, but there is another special one for them. The Pope and Young Club publishes a list of record trophies taken by bowhunters. Similar rules apply, but the minimums for whitetails are 125 points for typical and 135 for nontypical. Entry forms and more information are available from Pope and Young Records Office, 1804 Borah, Moscow, ID 83843. The biggest P&Y typical whitetail buck, scoring 204⁴/₈ points, was taken in Peoria County, Illinois in 1965. The number-one nontypical, from Hall County, Nebraska, in 1962, scored 279⅞.

There are many other trophy recognition programs operated by organizations such as Safari Club International, state and provincial agencies, and others.

Antler Mounts
While large trophies are often made into full head-and-shoulder mounts, hunters usually save only their buck's antlers. An antler

This diagram shows how to saw the skull plate if you wish to mount your buck's antlers. Extend cut number one past the eye sockets to the nose to save more skull plate for a "European" mount.

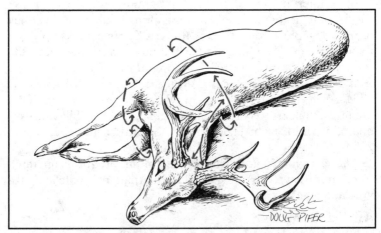

For a head and shoulders mount, bucks must be caped by making the cuts shown and skinning the front half of the deer.

mount is quick and inexpensive to make, and does not take up much space. Here's how to do it:

Remove the antlers by sawing off a bone plate from the skull at the antler base. With a hacksaw or other small-toothed saw, cut from about an inch behind the antlers angling downward to the top of the eye sockets. Cut across the bridge of the nose at the bottom of the eye sockets. Pry the skull plate loose.

Boil the skull plate until the hide and other tissues fall free from the bone. Do not let the antlers themselves submerge, or they will become discolored. Boil the skull plate again in clean water, remove, and submerge in cold water. The cold water will prevent grease from yellowing the bone later.

After the skull plate dries, it can be trimmed and mounted on a plaque with wood screws or epoxy. Some hunters prefer to cover the skull plate so only the antlers show. Leather, velvet, and plaster are favorite coverings.

Caping

Hunters often have a head mount made from large or otherwise special trophies. Head mounts include the neck or neck and shoulders, called the cape. Caping, or skinning the head/shoulders, must be done carefully to keep from damaging any detail that is to be preserved.

To remove the cape, cut completely around the buck's body ahead of the ribcage, then straight along the top of the back and neck between the first cut and a point just behind the antlers. From there, cut to and around each antler, and around each foreleg at the knee. Pull and cut the hide free, being very careful to keep the ears, nose, even the eyelashes on the hide. If you're unsure about your skinning ability, skin the neck and shoulders, cutting off the head to leave the detail work for the taxidermist.

If you can't get the cape immediately to a taxidermist, quick-freeze it or salt it well.

To ensure the mounted head looks like it did in life, take photographs from several angles before skinning the head and provide them to the taxidermist.

Other Deer Trophies

Tanned deer hides also make fine trophies. Hair-on whitetail skins are pretty wall hangings but constantly shed. With the hair removed, hides can be made into clothing and other items.

Some hunters make novelty items from deer forelegs. While

Photo by Joe Workosky

A skilled taxidermist can provide a lifelike mount that will last for years. Head-and-shoulder mounts cost about $150–300.

the joint is still pliable, secure the ankle into the right position to make a gunrack, lamp stand, or similar item.

Meat Handling

The quality of your venison depends on quick cooling and proper aging. Prompt, uniform cooling prevents spoilage and improves the flavor of meat. Allowing the carcass to age or "hang" in dry, cool air improves tenderness and taste.

In all situations, make sure the carcass is suspended to protect it from animals and to allow ventilation. Remove the tenderloins from inside the carcass to keep them from drying out. Prop open the body cavity to allow air to circulate. Immediately refrigerate the heart and liver.

Optimum handling of a deer carcass is to skin it immediately after it is killed and place it whole in a meat cooler. Skinning is much easier if done before the carcass loses all its body heat.

While many hunters leave the skin on their deer for several days before skinning and butchering, deer taken in warm weather should be skinned and cooled as soon as possible. Protect the

Photo by John Weiss

Venison should be cooled as soon as possible and kept cold throughout the aging process.

meat from moisture, but don't cover it with plastic — the meat must be ventilated. Keep insects off by wrapping the carcass with burlap or a similar covering, or by liberally sprinkling black pepper on the meat. If daytime temperatures are much over 50 degrees, the meat should not hang for more than a couple of days before it is butchered or hung in a meat cooler.

If temperatures stay below 50 degrees but not so cold that the meat alternately freezes and thaws, the carcass may be hung outside for several days with the skin on. Under optimum conditions — just above freezing — it may be aged for two weeks or more.

Skinning Deer

Deer are easiest to skin if they are hung just off the ground. They may be hung by the head or the back legs; the latter is recommended. Suspending the deer by each back leg makes it easier to skin and halve the carcass.

Begin by cutting around the knees and the insides of each leg between the knees and body. Lower legs may be removed by severing the ligaments at the joint or by sawing the bone just above the joint. Loosen the hide on the forelegs from the knees to the body. Cut off the tail, leaving it attached to the hide. The belly cut should extend from the anus to the jaw.

Pull the hide downward, cutting where necessary. Try to keep a thin covering of fat on the meat, but leave thick slabs of tallow on the hide rather than the carcass. Avoid getting hair on the meat. Cut the hide free when you reach the head.

One advantage of skinning a deer head-up is that you can hasten skinning by pulling the hide off with a vehicle. Make sure the deer is hung from a solid object with a strong rope, chain, or cable. After making the initial cuts, pull some hide away at the top of the neck. Secure this by rope to the front bumper of a car or truck; slowly back away. The hide should peel right off.

Butchering

Venison may be deboned and sliced into package-size pieces, or it may be sawed into cutlets like a butcher shop would. Deboning is faster and requires less equipment.

To debone venison, get a clean piece of paper or cloth on which to lay the pieces. Get a clean bucket or large pan to hold scraps of meat that are to be ground into hamburger.

Cut off each front quarter, then fillet the loins from the back-

Photo by Irene Vandermolen,
Rue Enterprises

Photo by Wade Bourne

Deer are easiest to skin if they are hung just off the ground, either head up or head down.

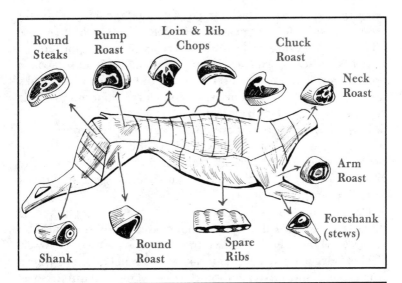

Round
Steaks

Rump
Roast

Loin & Rib
Chops

Chuck
Roast

Neck
Roast

Arm
Roast

Foreshank
(stews)

Shank

Round
Roast

Spare
Ribs

Some hunters cut up a deer the way beef is butchered, sawing bone as illustrated in the diagram above. Most debone their venison. Tenderloins, considered the best cut of venison, should be removed soon after field dressing.

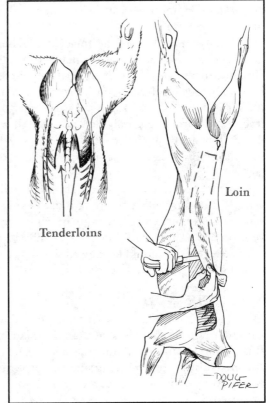

Tenderloins

Loin

—DOUG
PIFER

235

bone/ribcage. Remove each hind quarter and the neck. This will leave you with the ribcage and back, from which meat is removed for hamburger. Cut the loins into steaks and the quarters into roasts or steaks, whichever you prefer, and save all scraps for hamburger. Some people prefer to save only the choicest steaks and grind the rest into hamburger. Some of the hamburger meat can be cut into stew-size chunks.

If you have a meat saw and more time to spare, you can cut up your deer butcher-shop style. Halve the carcass by sawing down the center of the backbone. Cut the loin into chops, the ribs into spare ribs, and the quarters into bone-in steaks and roasts (see diagram).

Deer fat and tallow is bad-tasting and should be removed as much as possible. All hair, dirt, and clotted blood must also be removed. This is easiest by wiping it away with a paper towel.

Hamburger meat is usually taken to a butcher shop, where it is ground and mixed with pork (pure venison hamburger is rather dry). Hamburger can also be made at home with a grinder or food processor.

You may want to soak the meat in cold salt water for about 24 hours to reduce gaminess somewhat, but this isn't necessary. Chill the meat, wrap it in air-tight, meal-size portions, and freeze it quickly. Set the freezer on its coldest setting and spread the packages out. If stacked, the packages may take a long time to freeze and some meat may deteriorate. All packages should be dated. If you think the meat will be in the freezer for several months before it is eaten, it is best to double-wrap it in freezer paper.

Venison stored at 0 degrees Fahrenheit will keep for up to a year. If it is kept colder, there is more chance for freezer burn; warmer, and meat will deteriorate much faster. Ground or cubed venison has a shorter freezer life—usually less than six months.

Frozen venison should be thawed slowly in a refrigerator before cooking.

Cooking Venison

Deer meat has a higher nutritional value than domestic meat, with more protein and less fat than beef, lamb, pork, or poultry. It is high in vitamins and minerals and has no chemical additives. It is not subject to processing plant improprieties. And venison can be very delicious—depending on how it was handled and prepared.

When handled and prepared properly, venison is flavorful and high in nutrition. Be careful not to leave deer meat in the freezer or in the oven too long.

The palatability of venison depends on many factors. Venison from bucks and older deer is usually tougher. It is also tough if it has not been aged, and off-tasting if it was aged too long. Unsuspecting deer killed instantly are better tasting than deer that were chased or frightened. Stressed deer build up blood, adrenaline, and lactic acid in their muscles that causes the disagreeable "gamey" taste.

The main rule for cooking venison is don't overdo it. Venison has less fat and moisture than domestic meat so it dries out badly with overcooking. Venison is best if it is marinated and cooked with a moist-heat method. Roasts are best when cooked in a cooking bag with spices. When frying venison steaks or hamburgers, cook them quickly and remove them promptly.

Don't waste you deer's heart or liver; both are delicious. The heart can be portioned and fried in butter and seasoning like steak—it has a mild taste and pleasant texture. Venison liver has a naturally strong taste that can be removed by marinating it in milk overnight in the refrigerator. Then it is fried in onions like beef liver.

There are many good recipes for venison; a few are on the following page.

Venison Bacon Patties
1 lb. ground venison
½ lb. chopped bacon
1 chopped onion
1 egg
½ cup bread crumbs
1 tablespoon A-1 sauce

Mix all ingredients in a bowl and form patties. Fry or broil. Serve on hamburger buns.

Venison Stir Fry
2 lbs. frozen steak or roast
½ cup baby pea pods
1 8-oz. can water chestnuts
1 8-oz. can bean sprouts
½ cup thinly sliced carrots
¼ cup chopped onions
¼ cup chopped green peppers
2–4 cups rice

Slice meat as thinly as possible (this is easiest if it is only partially thawed). Heat fry pan or wok to 375 degrees; add olive or peanut oil. Cook rice separately. Add all other ingredients and cook until tender (20–30 minutes). Serve over rice; flavor with soy sauce.

Venison Sauerbraten
4–5 pound venison roast, deboned and trimmed of fat
3 cups chopped onions
3 cups water
3 cups dry red wine
1 cup cider vinegar
½ cup brown sugar
20 whole cloves
6 bay leaves
5 teaspoons salt
½ teaspoon pepper

Place roast and all ingredients in large glass bowl and mix. Refrigerate for 24 hours, turning the roast in the marinade occasionally. Remove meat from marinade, wipe dry, and brown in ¼ cup vegetable oil. Add marinade and bring to a boil. Reduce heat, cover, and simmer until meat is tender (about three hours) turning occasionally. Serve with potatoes, noodles, or rice.

CHAPTER 14

WHITETAIL HUNTING SAFETY AND ETHICS

There was a time when deer hunting was a perilous pastime. A half-century ago, dozens of deaths and injuries marred each deer season in the better deer hunting states. Just take a look at an old-time deer camp photo, and you can see why: Hunters are dressed in clothes as brown as the deer themselves. Just about every hunter has his rifle trained on another. Whiskey bottles often litter the campsite.

Times have changed—for the better. Even though there are more hunters concentrated on fewer hunting areas today, the

Photo by Mike Strandlund

Hunter education has led to a new awareness toward safety and ethics in hunting. Today's hunters are more safety conscious and conservation minded than ever before.

hunting accident rate has taken a phenomenal drop. A recent recreational safety study, rated the comparative risks of popular activities. From the most dangerous to the least dangerous, these activities included football, winter sports, baseball, bathing and swimming, basketball, skating, trips to the country or beach, bicycling, park activities, picnics, outings, golf, horseback riding, boating and canoeing, gymnasium activities, fishing, visits to the theater, church, or a concert, and (finally) hunting.

The increase in hunter safety is attributable to hunter safety laws, hunter education, and a general increase in awareness of safety afield. But even though deer hunting has become safer than many of the more "tame" activities, safety must not be taken for granted. Safe hunting depends on knowledge of the dangers and how to prevent them, constant awareness of dangerous situations, and responsible behavior afield.

In deer hunting, there are three types of safety that must be observed. These include gun safety, general outdoors safety, and deer hunting safety.

Gun Safety

The following safety rules apply to any type of situation in which a firearm is involved.

1. Always have control of the gun's muzzle and keep it pointed in a safe direction.
2. Be positive of your target's identity before shooting.
3. Be prepared and take time to fire a safe shot. If unsure, or if you must rush so you cannot mount the gun correctly, pass up the shot. If there is any doubt whether you should shoot–don't.
4. Use the right ammunition for your firearm. Carry only one type of ammo to ensure you don't mix different types. A 20-gauge shell loaded into a 12-gauge shotgun will slide into the barrel and lodge there. If a 12-gauge shell is loaded behind it and fired, the results can be disastrous. Be careful to use the right cartridge, powder, or projectile.
5. If you fall, control the muzzle. After a fall, unload and check for dirt and damage and make sure the barrel is free of obstructions.
6. Unload your gun before attempting to climb a steep bank or traveling across hazardous terrain.
7. When you are alone and must cross a fence, unload your firearm and place it under the fence with the muzzle

Having complete, conscious control of your gun is the foremost rule of hunting safety. Keep command of the muzzle, and unload any firearm before crossing an obstacle like a fence.

pointed away from your body. When hunting with others and you must cross a fence or similar obstacle, unload the gun and keep the action open. Have one of your companions hold the gun while you cross. Then take their unloaded guns so your companions may cross safely.

8. Maintain your firearm, keep it clean, and never use a gun that is in poor condition, malfunctioning, or incapable of handling the ammunition you use. In cold weather, remove oil and grease from the gun so it cannot congeal and inhibit the action.

9. Be aware of the range of your pellets or bullets. Buckshot and bullets can travel over a mile. Make certain that your pellets cannot rain down on other hunters, and remember that buckshot and bullets can ricochet off water, ground, and objects.

Photo by Mike Strandlund

Before pulling the trigger, be sure of your target and beyond. Never take a shot in which a misdirected bullet could travel toward unseen hunters or buildings.

Photo by Mike Strandlund

Eye and ear protection should be part of every session at the practice range.

10. Adverse conditions and excitement can impair your mental and physical performance. Bulky clothing, rain, wind, and snow can cause poor gun handling and reduce your concentration on safety. Fatigue can cause carelessness and clumsiness, as can the excitement of a deer approaching. For maximum safety, control these conditions as much as possible.

11. Be conscious of switching your gun's safety off, and remember to place it back on after the shooting opportunity has passed.

12. Establish zones of fire when hunting next to companions. Be sure your gun's muzzle is always pointing into your zone.

13. Alcohol, drugs, and hunting don't mix. Drugs and alcohol impair your judgment; keen judgment is essential to safe hunting.

14. When you have finished hunting, unload your gun immediately and keep the action open.

15. If companions violate a rule of safe gun handling, bring it to their attention and refuse to hunt with them unless they correct their behavior.

Hunters who use bows, muzzleloaders, or handguns have special safety rules to follow. Identifying the target and being sure of the background are also important before releasing an arrow. Broadheads must always be covered with an impenetrable shielding material such as a padded, hard-plastic guard on a bow quiver. When walking, especially on steep or otherwise hazardous terrain, bowhunters should keep all arrows quivered in most situations. A fall on a sharp broadhead can be as dangerous as a gunshot wound.

Muzzleloader hunters must be especially careful when loading their rifles. Black powder, erroneously considered

Photo by Mike Strandlund

Muzzleloader hunters have many special safety considerations. Learn all about muzzleloading before you begin to shoot, and keep safety foremost in your mind.

by some to be a tame pro-
pellent, can cause a violent
breech explosion with improper
loads. Common causes of accidents include exceeding maximum powder charges; acci-
dently loading double charges
of powder and ball; using
smokeless powder or black
powder that is too fine; and
others.

If you're a handgunner, you
must remember that the handgun's short barrel makes it
more liable to point at yourself
or someone else. Keep the gun
securely holstered with the safety on, and be especially careful
when moving the gun into or
out of the holster. The hammer
of a revolver should rest on an
empty chamber.

Photo by Mike Strandlund

**Because of the short barrel, muz-
zle control is more difficult with a
handgun than with a rifle. Take
extra precautions with pistols and
revolvers.**

Safety Afield

Many of the safety concerns a deer hunter must remember have
nothing to do with guns. In fact, deer hunters are more likely
to be hurt in an incident *not* involving a gun or bow. They include the ever-present dangers of being in the woods: falls and
similar mishaps, hypothermia, sickness, drowning, thirst, and
starvation.

Being careful and "staying found" will prevent most of these.
Use common sense; keep safety in mind. Always carry maps and
a compass if there is a possibility of getting lost (even in familiar
country) and know how to use them. Make sure that someone
knows where you are going and when you plan to be back. Carry
a first-aid kit, maybe a snake-bite kit, and signalling devices.

Hypothermia, or severe loss of body heat, is a little-understood
affliction. It is one of the biggest threats to the outdoorsman,
possible in temperatures as warm as 60 degrees under certain
conditions. Wet clothes, wind, and fatigue contribute to
hypothermia.

Persons suffering from hypothermia go through stages beginning with shivering and progressing to loss of muscular control,

"Staying found" will prevent getting lost and related predicaments. Use a compass, and mark your way in the woods.

mental confusion, and unconsciousness. Victims may have very pale skin, rigid muscles, and may be unable to speak.

To help prevent hypothermia, wear clothes that offer good protection in wind and wet, such as rainsuits or nylon shell jackets, combined with wool or good synthetic insulation. Dress in layers. If you think there is a good chance of getting wet, you should bring a change of dry clothes in a waterproof bag. Don't overexert yourself, as tiredness lowers resistance to cold. Take precautions from getting wet. Carry sources of heat, such as warm drinks in thermos bottles, fire-building material, camp stoves, etc.

Hypothermia victims often don't realize the seriousness of the situation. They should be warmed with blankets, warm water, hot drinks, or the body heat of companions.

Rugged terrain presents a variety of hazards to the hunter. There is the possibility of a fall. There is the chance that an older or out-of-shape hunter could become exhausted and have a heart

Photo by Gerald Almy

Improper clothing for the conditions is the leading cause of hypothermia. Cotton clothing is the worst if you get wet; wool and polypropylene are best.

attack. The danger of these situations is compounded because hunters are often far from help and by themselves.

In some areas, poisonous snakes, rabid animals, wood ticks carrying Lyme Disease, and other dangerous animals may pose a threat. Learn about these dangers, and take precautions.

Remember the best preventions for all problems afield are planning and common sense.

Deer Hunting Safety

The combination of high-power rifles, large numbers of hunters, limited visibility in woods, and other factors can create dangerous situations. There are special safety considerations for whitetail hunters:

- Always wear an ample amount of blaze orange. Even if only a blaze orange hat is required, you should have more

Photo by Wade Bourne

A hunter dragging a deer is an unsafe situation. Make sure you have ample blaze orange clothing while dragging deer.

orange on the lower part of your body. When a hunter is shot by another because he is mistaken for a deer, it is often because the shooter saw only the victim's dull-colored legs moving through brush. Wear blaze orange pants or tie a piece of orange material around each leg. If you don't want to wear more than the minimum amount of blaze orange, supplement it with bright red clothing. This is almost as visible to other hunters, yet appears gray to deer. If you are bowhunting in camo clothing, wear a piece of blaze orange when walking to and from your stand.

- Use a flashlight when moving through woods in darkness or twilight. This is the time when most accidents occur. If you have a flashlight, no one can mistake you for a deer. A light also helps prevent injuries from a fall or other accident.

- When field-dressing or taking a deer from the woods, keep orange clothing visible. There is a tendency for hunters to remove their coats when doing these duties. They must be kept prominent, however, because this is one of the most dangerous times of the hunt.

Photos by Mike Strandlund

Tree stands are a leading cause of accidents among hunters. Climb carefully into the stand without trying to carry gear with you. Immediately attach a safety belt, and then bring up your equipment with a haul line.

- Use extreme care when hunting from tree stands. When getting into or out of your stand, momentarily clear your mind of deer hunting and everything else but safety. Tree stand accidents have surpassed gun accidents and have become the most dangerous part of deer hunting. Always use a safety harness when entering, leaving, and sitting in a tree stand. Unload your gun, cover your broadheads, and use a haul line to get them into and out of the stand. Check the stand and steps periodically to make sure they are in good condition, and be careful to install them securely. Some designs of portable tree stands are much safer than others. Never use a portable stand that is hung only from a single bolt or spike imbedded in the tree trunk.
- Never substitute a rifle scope for binoculars.
- Never shoot at sound or movement. Assume every sound you hear and movement you see is another hunter until proven otherwise. Never point your gun, take the safety off, or put your finger on the trigger until you have positively identified the target as the game you want to shoot.
- Disregard peer pressure that places such urgent importance on getting a deer that it causes you to take chances.

- Be aware of buck fever and its prevention. Close encounters with big bucks (or even small does) can cause the extreme excitement that causes accidents. Anyone is capable of blunders at the sight of a buck. Anticipation can make you see something that is not there. Chances of this are increased if the hunter is inexperienced, fatigued, or has poor eyesight. Ambitious hunters are tempted to take risks. But the right attitude, with safety foremost, greatly reduces the odds of a mishap.
- When hunting with companions, be certain of each other's location.
- If you're on land where you have sole permission to hunt, don't assume there are no other hunters around. That attitude may prompt you to take chancy shots.
- Avoid areas with high hunting pressure.
- Remember that poachers and other irresponsible hunters may be nearby. Take every possible precaution — never assume that other hunters are safe.

NRA Staff Photo

Whitetail hunters who try to attract bucks by rattling and calling must be especially careful, because they may also attract other hunters.

Deer Hunting Ethics

Hunting ethics encompass all the responsibilities a hunter has to other hunters, landowners, the general public, and the game. Governments require certain generally accepted ethical behavior through hunting laws and regulations. But in most cases, it is up to the hunter to decide what is right and what is wrong, and to hunt according to those standards.

Some ethical questions in deer hunting are easy to answer. If you are hunting a bucks-only zone, you simply do not point your gun until you see a deer with antlers.

Other ethical questions are tough. A huge buck is making a getaway. Do you risk taking a shot, knowing you may wound but not recover him? Suppose you do connect and he enters property posted *No Trespassing*. Should you go in after him?

The ethical standards of hunters cover a wide range. A few hunters believe it is only sporting to hunt trophy bucks, one-on-one, with a bow and arrow from the ground. On the other end of the spectrum are hunters who believe they have an ethical right to use dogs, drivers, buckshot, and even vehicles and walkie-talkies to hunt deer—including does and fawns. Who can say who is right?

Most ethical questions can be resolved by answering these questions: Is it legal or, is it fair to everyone concerned, including the game, other people, and myself? There are laws and standards to follow, but ultimately, you must decide.

Photo by Mike Strandlund

Deer hunters are faced with many ethical dilemmas. You must consider other people, the game, and yourself when deciding what is right.

Responsibility to Other Hunters

Besides safety, you have several other responsibilities to fellow hunters. If you find another hunter at the place you planned to make a deer stand, bow out and find another site. It is counter-productive to challenge him to the spot, and in deer hunting, you have to be first. Hopefully, another hunter will someday show you the same respect.

Try to pass on responsible hunting behavior to fellow hunters. If a new hunter seems to be going astray, try to educate him in hunting ethics. If a companion refuses to hunt responsibly, refuse to hunt with him.

Don't litter, drive vehicles where others may be hunting, or otherwise disturb other people or the area. Most hunters have deep feelings for nature and the peace of mind they find while hunting. Don't violate them.

Responsibilities to Landowners

One example of how hunters hurt themselves through poor ethics is the alienation of landowners. Each year, thousands of acres of private land are posted off-limits because hunters treated the land or its owner with disrespect. It hurts all hunters.

Always get permission before hunting on any private property. Approach the landowner with courtesy—not only because you will have a better chance of getting permission, but because

Photo by Mike Strandlund

Always get permission before hunting on private land, and once there, treat the property with the utmost respect.

we all have a responsibility to promote the image of the good sportsman. Once you receive permission, treat the land with utmost care. Leave no signs you were there — take spent shells and litter with you, and maybe pick up some left by others. Don't drive on soft ground and leave tire ruts.

Other ways to keep good landowner relations are to avoid disturbing livestock, fences, crops, and other property. Don't abuse your welcome by bringing a carload of companions or hunting on the land day after day.

A token of appreciation such as a gift, a card, or offer to help with chores goes a long way toward being welcome next year.

Responsibilities to the Public

Remember that the environment and animals belong to everyone, not just hunters. Respect the rights of people who enjoy nature without hunting — avoid shooting in areas where you know nonhunters are enjoying the outdoors. Keep shell cases, gut piles, and other signs of hunting out of view. Don't display bagged animals to people who may not want to see them. Remember that unfavorable public opinion has resulted in laws and regulations that have hurt hunters.

Another duty the hunter owes the public is to ensure the enforcement of all laws. Hunters must abide by the laws and report those who trespass, poach animals, shoot road signs, or otherwise vandalize property.

Photos by Mike Strandlund

When you kill a whitetail or any other wild animal, you have a responsibility to find, tag, recover, and utilize the game.

A conscientious hunter studies nature and gains an intimate knowledge of the outdoors. More than anyone else he appreciates the joyous beauty of life and the harsh inevitability of death among wildlife.

Responsibilities to the Game

The whitetail deer is more than a resource to be harvested. It is a magnificent wild animal, one of nature's most wondrous creations. Deer and all game animals deserve the greatest respect a hunter can give his prey. Hunters who do not feel a deep reverence for the whitetail and an obligation to conserve the resource are missing the essence of hunting.

Never take a shot that has a better chance of crippling than killing. Don't shoot at deer beyond your accurate range and don't shoot at running deer that are near-impossible to hit. Don't shoot at a deer if another deer is standing directly behind it—the bullet could kill the first deer and wound the second. Always look for antlers before shooting in a bucks-only zone.

Help in the conservation and propagation of deer. You'll help conserve and promote deer hunting in the process.

Responsibilities to Yourself

Finally, don't forget your responsibilities to yourself. Learn all you can to improve your deer hunting skills and safety. The NRA, wildlife agencies, and other organizations offer courses to enhance your ability and enjoyment of hunting, as well as your safety.

If a certain law or hunting regulation conflicts with your well-considered ethical beliefs, work to change that law. Fight it with letters and votes, not disobedience.

Don't take a chance or violate your ethics in a way you may regret later. At the same time, hunt hard, hunt honestly, and be proud of your sportsmanship.

Pass Along the Tradition

If you're a hunter in the truest sense, you will eventually reach a point where you derive the most hunting satisfaction from introducing others to the sport. It may be acquainting a friend with hunting, taking a young boy or girl on their first hunt, or volunteering in a hunter education program.

Talk with the new hunter about hunting responsibilities and ethics that all hunters should abide. Show respect for game by never taking a chancy shot, by making every effort to recover a wounded animal, and by never wasting bagged game. Make him or her realize why they must also treat landowners and the general public with respect, to prevent prejudice against hunters. Instruct new hunters early on safety, ethics and responsibility, because their respect and appreciation of the sport will determine the future of hunting.

Photos by Mike Strandlund

To perpetuate our hunting heritage, we must pass on our love of hunting and the outdoors. Teach your children well, and get involved in a local hunter safety or hunter education program.

Appendix

257

THE NRA AND HUNTING

The National Rifle Association encourages and supports sport hunting through a wide variety of programs and services.

The NRA Hunter Services Division assists state and provincial hunter education programs with support materials and training programs for professional and volunteer staff. NRA Hunter Clinics answer the demand for advanced education by emphasizing skills, responsibility, and safety as applied to hunting techniques and game species. The Hunter Information Service communicates to the members a variety of information necessary to plan and complete hunts. The NRA Youth Hunter Education Challenge offers a series of events on the local, state, and national levels to challenge young hunters, through hunting-simulated events, to apply basic skills learned in the classroom. The NRA Hunter Recognition Program offers awards to hunters for all levels of hunting achievement. Financial support for wildlife management and shooting sports research is available through the NRA Grants-in-Aid Program.

The NRA Institute for Legislative Action protects the legal rights of hunters. NRA publications provide a variety of printed material on firearms, equipment and techniques for hunters, including *American Hunter* magazine, the largest periodical in the U.S. devoted to hunting. Junior programs encourage young people to participate in hunting. Special insurance benefits are available to NRA hunting members, and hunters can further benefit by joining an NRA hunting club or by affiliating an existing club with the NRA. The NRA works with other hunting organizations to sustain a positive image of hunting as a traditional form of recreation, to combat anti-hunting efforts, and to promote a life-long interest in hunting.

For further information, contact the Hunter Services Division, National Rifle Association, 1600 Rhode Island Avenue, N.W., Washington, D.C. 20036. (1-202-828-6240)

NRA MATERIALS FOR THE WHITETAIL DEER HUNTER

The following are materials available from the NRA Sales Department and can help you prepare your next hunt.

Description	Item No.	Unit Price
The Hunter's Guide	HE5N5090	$ 8.95 each
NRA Hunter Skills Series		
Student Manuals		
Whitetail Deer Hunting	HS5N5305	$ 5.00 each
Bow Hunting	HS5N5403	$ 5.00 each
Muzzleloader Hunting	HS5N5145	$ 5.00 each
Western Big Game Hunting	HS5N5207	$ 5.00 each
Waterfowl Hunting	HS5N5083	$ 5.00 each
Wild Turkey Hunting	HS5N5707	$ 5.00 each

Note: Discount prices for quantity purchases are available for the above titles.

Hardbound Versions		
Whitetail Deer Hunting	HS5N5261	$14.95 each
Bowhunting	HS5N5549	$14.95 each
Muzzleloader Hunting	HS5N5172	$14.95 each
Wild Turkey Hunting	HS5N5734	$14.95 each

NRA Hunter Clinic Video (VHS) Collection		
Brochure/		
Order Form	HS3N5003	N/C
Successful Whitetail Deer Hunting	HS5N7063	$19.95 each
Way of the Whitetail	HS5N7045	$19.95 each
Bowhunting for Whitetail Deer	HS5N7081	$19.95 each
Formula for Success: Deer Hunting	HS5N7143	$19.95 each
Formula for Success:		
Bowhunting for Deer	HS5N7152	$19.95 each
The Elusive Whitetail	HS5N7125	$19.95 each
Bowhunting for Trophy Whitetails	HS5N7205	$19.95 each
Strategies for Finding Trophy Bucks	HS5N7214	$19.95 each
Stalking Trophy Bucks	HS5N7223	$19.95 each
Hunter Clinic Program		
Brochure–		
Keeping the Tradition Alive		
and Flourishing!	HS3N0053	N/C
NRA Hunter Clinic Instructor		
Certification Order Form	HS3N8037	N/C
Hunter Orange Cap (Winter)	HS5N2148	$ 5.00 each
Brown Camouflage Cap (Summer)	HS5N3012	$ 5.00 each
Trebark Camouflage Cap (Summer)	HS5N3129	$ 5.00 each

Description	Item No.	Unit Price
Hunter Clinic Patch	HS5N2022	$ 1.00 each
Hunter Clinic Lapel Pin	HS5N6206	$ 2.00 each

Note: Additional promotional items and instructor support materials are available.

NRA Hunter Recognition Awards		
Brochure	HI3N0106	N/C
Young Deer Hunter Award		
Brassard	HI5N2157	$ 1.00 each
Whitetail Deer Lapel Pin	HI5N6117	$ 3.00 each
Life-Size Game Targets Brochure	HS3N0017	N/C
Whitetail Deer (set of 5)	HS5N1425	$ 5.00 each
Whitetail Deer (set of 50)	HS5N1434	$40.00 each
One Each Target (set of 13)	HS5N1023	$ 7.00 each

Package containing one each: Whitetail Deer, Turkey, Duck, Rabbit, Groundhog, Mule Deer, Black Bear, Pronghorn, Javelina, Coyote, Red Fox, Pheasant, and Squirrel

Note: Package quantities of 5 or 50 are available for all game targets listed above.

Other Brochures		
Whitetail Tips	HI3N0017	N/C
Wild Game From Field to Table	HI3N0080	N/C
Firearm Safety and the Hunter	HE3N0122	N/C
The Hunter and Wildlife	HI3N0071	N/C
Landowner Relations	HE3N0033	N/C
Responsible Hunting	HE3N0024	N/C
Hypothermia	HE3N0079	N/C
Fitness and Nutrition	HE3N0097	N/C
Water Safety	HE3N0051	N/C
Tree Stand Safety	HE3N0015	N/C
Hunting's Future? It's Up to You	HE3N0159	N/C
NRA and Hunting	HI3N0115	N/C
NRA Hunter Services Division Materials		
Price List	HI3N8091	N/C
NRA Standard Order Form	XS7N8000	N/C

ORDERING INFORMATION

- Use the NRA Standard Order Form to order items listed. Prices are subject to change without notice.
- Prices do not include shipping and handling charges. Certain state sales taxes are applicable.
- Order forms and current prices are available from NRA Sales Department, P.O. Box 5000, Kearneysville, WV 25430-5000 or call **toll free 1-800-336-7402**. VA residents call **toll free 1-800 535-9982**. Hours: 9:00 a.m. to 5:00 p.m. Eastern time.

THE NRA HUNTER SKILLS SERIES

T he NRA Hunter Skills Series is a developing library of books on hunting, shooting, and related activities. It supports the NRA Hunter Clinic Program, a national network of seminars conducted by the NRA Hunter Services Division and volunteer hunter clinic instructors.

The hunter training manuals are developed by NRA staff, with the assistance of noted hunting experts, hunter educators, experienced outdoor writers, and representatives of hunting/conservation organizations. The publications are available in student (bound) and instructor (loose leaf) editions.

The program is planned to include clinics and support material on hunting whitetail deer, waterfowl, wild turkey, small game, predators, upland game, western big game, and others. It will also address marksmanship and hunting with rifle, shotgun, muzzleloader, handgun, and archery equipment.

For more information about the NRA Hunter Clinic Program and its training materials, contact NRA Hunter Services Division, 1600 Rhode Island Avenue, N.W., Washington, D.C. 20036. Phone (202) 828-6240.

NRA BIG GAME HUNTER AWARDS

Let the NRA Big Game Hunter Awards Program help preserve the excitement and memories of some of your best hunts. This program emphasizes the hunter's skills and quality of the hunt—not trophy size. The minimum requirements for all 14 categories of North American big game that are accepted for these awards are listed in the chart below. The program recognizes achievement in four different hunting methods:

Modern Firearm—Long Gun
Modern Firearm—Handgun
Muzzleloading Firearm
Bow and Arrow

Beautifully designed certificates mounted on walnut plaques are personalized with the hunt method, hunter's name, animal category and the year and the state or province of the hunt.

Requirements

Category	Index for Determining Status	Minimum Requirements
Whitetail Deer	Minimum numbers	4
Coues Whitetail Deer	of points	3
Elk	on at least	5
Mule Deer	one side	4
Black-tailed Deer	of rack	3
Black Bear	Greatest width plus	16 inches
Cougar	length of skull	12 inches
Grizzly Bear or Brown Bear	without jaw	18 inches
Moose	Greatest spread	40 inches
Caribou	Maximum inside spread	30 inches
Pronghorn	Length of	11 inches
Rocky Mountain Goat	longest horn	8 inches
Native Wild Sheep	Extent of curl	¾
Wild Turkey	Beard length	8 inches

For more information on the NRA Big Game Hunter Awards refer to the NRA Hunter Recognition Program brochure (HI3N0106) or contact the National Rifle Association of America, Hunter Services Division, 1600 Rhode Island Avenue, N.W., Washington, D.C. 20036-3268. Telephone (202) 828-6240.